no excuse

LIZ LOCHHEAD

no excuse, but honestly
it's hard to draw
Jura's beauty –
foxgloves and fuchsia far too flashy for
just black and white
hard to write –
the mountains with their purple passages
the long curve of empty road
the wide swathe of empty moor
the too-blue-for-Scotland sky
this
intricacy of thistles
far too intent on being emblematic

Dedicated to Sir Bernard Crick,
Orwell's biographer, 1929–2008.

SPIRIT OF JURA

Fiction, Essays and Poems from the Jura Lodge

John Burnside
Bernard Crick
Janice Galloway
Philip Gourevitch
Romesh Gunesekera
Kathleen Jamie
Liz Lochhead
Swetha Prakash
Will Self

Edited by
Marc Lambert

Drawings
David Faithfull

First published in 2009 by Polygon,
an imprint of Birlinn Ltd

West Newington House
10 Newington Road
Edinburgh
EH9 1QS

9 8 7 6 5 4 3 2 1

www.birlinn.co.uk

The publishers acknowledge support from the following sponsors.

ISBN 978 1 84697 128 0

British Library Cataloguing-in-Publication Data
A catalogue record for this book is available on request
from the British Library.

Typeset by Koinonia, Manchester
Printed and bound by
CPI Antony Rowe, Chippenham, Wiltshire

Contents

KATHLEEN JAMIE — Approaching Jura — 3

KATHLEEN JAMIE — Pier in the morning — 11

JANICE GALLOWAY — Almost 1948 — 13

KATHLEEN JAMIE — Evans Walk — 21

BERNARD CRICK — Orwell on Jura — 23

KATHLEEN JAMIE — The gardener's shed — 33

ROMESH GUNESEKERA — Superstition — 35

LIZ LOCHHEAD — Cornucopia — 43

SWETHA PRAKASH — Shadows — 49

DAVID FAITHFULL — Dih-rah: oak gall landscapes — 59

JOHN BURNSIDE — Deer Island — 75

PHILIP GOUREVITCH — Enough — 81

KATHLEEN JAMIE — Evening — 89

JOHN BURNSIDE — The Deer Larder — 91

KATHLEEN JAMIE — Corran sands — 109

WILL SELF — Tissue Sample — 111

LIZ LOCHHEAD — Twenty One Year Old — 125

The Whiskies

CHARLES MACLEAN — Whisky Distilling on the Island of Deer — 131

RICHARD PATERSON — Spirit of the Island — 141

v

CONTENTS

Coda

LIZ LOCHHEAD   Some Things I Covet
                     in the Jura Lodge   145

Biographies   147
Acknowledgements   151

Spirit of Jura

INTRODUCTION

It had been pouring all day and the gulls were laughing.

So begins 'Almost 1948', Janice Galloway's pitch-perfect fictional account of a brief moment in Orwell's life on Jura, where he settled, in April 1946, to write what was first called *The Last Man In Europe*, and which finally became *Nineteen Eighty-Four*. 'I am anxious to get out of London for my own sake,' he wrote. 'I want to write another book which is impossible unless I can get six months' quiet . . .'

As Orwell's most distinguished biographer, the late Sir Bernard Crick, tells us in his essay 'Orwell on Jura', Jura was just the place for him. In 1946 it was almost 'unget-at-able', a sparsely populated island thirty miles long and seven wide, covered in blanket bog and featuring some of the wildest, most glorious landscapes in the British Isles. It is not much different today.

Inevitably, with such a heritage, the idea of the Jura Malt Whisky Writer Retreat programme began with Orwell and what he achieved in the solitude of Barnhill, the remote house he rented at the northern end of the island. It is fitting therefore that, in the space of two short years, the programme has established itself as a major addition to the literary landscape of Britain. Time and time again, the chosen writers, installed for a month in the uncanny luxuriousness of the Jura distillery lodge, have returned bearing the gifts that flow from uninterrupted creative time. The evidence is not just in books such as Will Self's *The Butt*, Philip Gourevitch's *Standard Operating Procedure* or Janice Galloway's *This Is Not About Me*, but in the numerous articles, poems and stories which the experience of the island, in one way or another, has provoked.

And here is the evidence: from Liz Lochhead's expansive love and laughter-filled lines to Kathleen Jamie's exquisitely observed poems of nature and landscape; from Romesh Gunesekera's love story – an oblique homage to the incredible Jura House gardens – to John Burnside's darker, ghostly imaginings in poem and prose, utterly rooted in the island but written with a nod to Maupassant and Pound; from Philip Gourevitch's meditation on isolation and loss, both physical and mental, to Will Self's story about a story, which unfolds like a nest of Russian dolls; and finally from Swetha Prakash's melding of an Eastern sensibility into the stuff of Jura's landscape to David Faithfull's drawings, the fruit of many years spent observing the unrivalled panoramas of the Scottish islands.

Truly, Jura is a place where nature, geography, history – and one of Scotland's finest whiskies – come together to make a vividly inspirational setting. To echo Will Self, nothing in this creative economy is ever lost. Settle down with this book and a glass of Jura malt, and see if it works for you too.

Marc Lambert
CEO, Scottish Book Trust

Approaching Jura

KATHLEEN JAMIE

If you take the ferry from the Scottish mainland to Port Askaig, on Islay, you'll sail out of West Loch Tarbet, westward into the wide Sound of Jura, and if you've a passing interest in landscape or wildlife, it's well worth pulling on a warm jacket, finding a space out of the wind and staying up on deck.

The crossing takes two hours. You're not out in the open sea. Ahead is land, the higher tops hidden under cloud as often as not. But over the water there'll be gannets, gleaming as they dive, and, low above the waves, the now-black, now-white flick of Manx shearwaters. You might be lucky and catch sight of porpoises, or maybe, in summer, the black fin of a basking shark.

At length, the ferry enters the narrow Sound of Islay, and for several long miles on the northern starboard side, you sail by the southern coast of Jura, barely a half mile away. This is a lovely sail. You pass small empty beaches, above them long plains of peat and bracken, and a few pine plantations. Some miles inland rise the three rounded, scree-grey hills called the Paps of Jura. If it's clear, you can see that they are breast-like, rounded, not jagged, and not especially high, less than 3,000 feet, but as the traveller Martin Martin put it mildly in 1695, 'they are very conspicuous from all quarters of sea and land in those parts'.

My most recent visit was in mid September, the very last days of summer. As we sailed through the narrow Sound, I was standing at the front of the ferry. A Yorkshireman next to me said, 'Is that Jura?'

'Yes,' I said. We looked at the miles of peat moor, a line of telegraph poles marching their lonely way. Two deer grazed on a seaward slope.

'Looks fantastic. Just nothing. I like that. Fantastic nothing.'

But nothing is nothing.

Jura is an island, but not 'remote', and not round, and not pelagic. That is to say, it's not a far flung dot in the ocean. It's one of a chain of islands, the southern Inner Hebrides, long inhabited and tucked in close to the Scottish mainland. One doesn't go 'up' to Jura – it lies on the same latitude as Glasgow, Falkirk, Edinburgh; Scotland's populous Central Belt.

On the map it resembles an elongated teardrop, with its weighty mountains down at the southern end. It would be a strong shape were it not almost split in two. There is a place in the middle of the island where the Atlantic finds its way, via a long finger of a loch, to within a mile of the east coast. 'Tarbert' is a common place-name in Scotland because that's what it means, in Gaelic – a portage, an isthmus narrow enough to carry a boat over, from the days when all communication would have been by boat, and the land a trackless obstacle. But today there are roads.

The ferry docked, and disgorged its traffic, which dispersed mostly onto populous Islay, but if you're going to Jura you must take another, much smaller vessel, which carries six vehicles at a pinch, takes five minutes to make its journey, and reaches a slipway where there is one building, some grazing cattle and precisely four street lamps. From there a single track road, *the* road, a road with grass and wild flowers growing in its middle, sets off eastward over a moor. The next street lamps were eight miles away, in the village, *the* village, of Craighouse. I took to the road, and met three vehicles on the way. A postie's van, the island's minibus, and an expensive Land-Rover, belonging, presumably, to one of the estates into which the island is divided. Whenever I pulled into a passing place, to allow the other vehicles by, always with a wave, I got out of the car to listen to the silence of the moor, and have a look at the hills.

I only had a couple of days, and had hoped to climb a Pap, for the sake of the view, but the summits were obscured by low surly cloud, and experience told me it would be much more wet up there than it looked. When I stopped to let the minibus by, I saw a hen harrier flying low over the moor a quarter mile away, following a line of fence posts. Within ten minutes of leaving the ferry slipway, I'd seen two hen harriers and a short-eared owl, as well as deer.

The village of Craighouse is on the island's sheltered east side. Here are the hotel, the Jura Stores and the distillery – all whitewashed. Out in the bay lie three calm little islands. A couple of yachts were moored, on water that lay like silk. The air smelled, not unpleasantly, of whisky.

Above the fireplace in the restaurant in the small hotel, there is a framed exhibit. It shows microliths – tiny worked pieces of flint, blades and scrapers, some no bigger than a fingernail. These had been discovered on the island and were 8,000 years old, thus proving that Jura had been inhabited, or perhaps in those Mesolithic days visited seasonally, for a very long time. People would have taken fish and deer and wild boar. When traveller Martin Martin came by in 1695, he wrote that Jura was 'perhaps the wholesomest plot of ground either in the isles or continent of Scotland'. People lived to a ripe old age. At its height, before the days of nineteenth-century emigration the population topped 1,200. (They say there were no forced evictions, as happened elsewhere.) Nowadays, only 200 people live here. What do they do? There is a doctor, a school, the distillery, five estates with estate workers and stalkers. There are a few crofters. (By chance I met a crofter, I gave him a lift because he was running up the road after his errant sheep. He told me he was one of very few indigenous Jura folk on the island and that many of the houses are holiday homes left empty all winter. Jura is not alone in that.) There is an airstrip, and a beautiful walled garden, with a gardener; the island has its very own takeaway van. Sometimes they do a venison korma. Except on special occasions, like the music festival, there are no police. Many of the residents are recent incomers, after a different sort of life to that they led in the south. The hotel bar is the hub of the place, but you won't hear Gaelic spoken. There's a village hall.

After supper I took a stroll through the village, down to the pier. Outside the village hall I found a noticeboard where the proceedings of the Community Council were posted. What troubles the people of Jura now? As on all small islands there is much concern with communications and ferries. There's an issue about mobile phone signals, or lack of, and the state of a certain sewage outfall. And deer. A problem had arisen with deer wandering into town. 'The stags can intimidate people,' the council noted. 'Stags can be unpredictable.'

They say Jura means Island of Deer. The human population is held to this narrow coastal strip along the sheltered east side, leaving the miles-long Atlantic coast without human habitation, but thick with Gaelic names, and in-between, anything up to eight miles of fabulous nothing, hills and bogs and lochans, that's the deer's place.

And that's where I'd hoped to go, a day's hike over the moor, up onto the tops, but in the morning, though the sea was bright, and the coast mellow, cloud still clamped down on the hills, down to about 700 feet. Not much good for hillwalking. I thought I'd explore the road, see if the cloud lifted later in the day.

The road, as I say, clings to the coast, sometimes swooping high through pine plantations, sometimes at sea-level, skirting the top of quiet bays. From Craighouse it runs a further twenty miles north, grass in the middle, in various states of repair. After that, it becomes a mere track, and when that peters out, for the few miles left, to the island's northernmost end, you walk.

Why would you make that trek, through damp bracken, with adders, to the northernmost tip of the island? Because you would pass the farm where George Orwell took himself to write *Nineteen Eighty-Four*, and farther, because at the island's northern tip, as the tide surges between Jura and the next island, Scarba, you can look down on the great whirlpool of Corryvreckan, suppurating and peaking. But that was for another day.

I drove up the road, stopping frequently in passing places. At the shore, soft and pleasant, the fuchsia was in bloom and rowan berries hung red, and there was purple knapweed in the ditches. All that had a sweet, mellow atmosphere. But immediately inland the land rose into peat-bog and scree-covered hill, topped by that shifting grey cloud. All the time on Jura I had an odd, lopsided feeling, of clinging to an edge. That high hinterland had great presence, both forbidding and inviting.

Sometimes an ivory gleam appeared in a saddle between the hills, then the cloud returned. Once, the summit of Beinn Shiantaidh appeared briefly through the cloud, but only briefly. I've heard, though I don't know if it's true, that you can see the Paps of Jura from the high-rise flats in Glasgow. It ought not to be so wild, being so close to a big city, but it is.

I decided to remain at the sunlit coast.

Farther up the coast, the road swoops and climbs, now giving sea views, now in the shade of trees. At one moment I had in sight, all at once, a stag on a hillside, a kestrel in the air, and a lighthouse out at sea, standing on a rock no bigger than itself.

Later in the afternoon – a soft drizzle had set in – I left the car in a passing place, and wandered down a track to the little-used jetty at Luss. The jetty is at the edge of a bay. The water – it was half-tide – gleamed in the soft light, so did the swirls of mustard-coloured wrack on the stones.

I didn't notice the stag at first. He was kneeling quietly not twenty yards away from the track – it was his rack of antlers sticking up I saw first. Keeping a wary eye on him, I carried on past, down to the jetty.

Something was disturbing the surface of the water. An otter. Jura has a great population of otters. Quietly, I sat on a rock to watch it. When it swam, the otter pushed the seawater into a little pressure wave over the bridge of its nose. Then it went under, head, back, sleek tail lifting last of all, and a trail of bubbles rose. After a moment, it surfaced, with something in its jaws, like a grotesque moustache. A green crab. Then the otter came ashore, and among the damp bladderwrack, not fifty yards away, began to eat. The stag, under his antlers, paid me no heed. He was looking out to sea as though in a dream.

I thought, this is ridiculously silent. It's a Saturday afternoon. Imagine Oxford Street, Sauchiehall Street. Here was a bay, with wooded hills behind, a stag kneeling among the bracken and, bar myself, not a human soul. The only sound in the whole world was an otter's fierce little teeth crunching through a crab shell.

The otter disposed of the crab, then nosed among the weed for any bits it had dropped. Then I jumped, startled. A bellowing roar had come from high on the hill above the bay and the sound echoed out over the silent water. The stag at my right paused for a long moment, shifted a little, then felt obliged to bellow in return. Mid-September, it was coming to the rutting season. Soon they'd all be at it. The sound must be tremendous.

'Stags can be unpredictable.' If I was between two, both with their dander up, maybe it was time to tiptoe away. Anyway, my mind had been wandering back to Craighouse, and venison korma, and then perhaps an evening drink and a conversation in the bar. The otter slipped back into the water. I hadn't climbed my hill, and had to go home tomorrow. No matter. It would wait for another time.

Pier in the morning

KATHLEEN JAMIE

Rain falls softly, puckering the sea.
The small isles are ghostly in mist.

Moored to an orange buoy
a rusty fishing boat from Ullapool.

Bottle-bank, public lavatory, stack of lobster creels.
When will anyone wake?

Almost 1948

JANICE GALLOWAY

It had been pouring all day and the gulls were laughing.

He could see them wheeling over the rocks. Wet to the bone, the neck of his oilskin streaming, he settled the motorbike against the roughcast wall of the stores. Someone, he knew, would be watching from inside. *Here's Mr Blair with his toothbrush moustache all set to drip over the dry goods. He is cadaverously thin.* Not that they ever said such things out loud, but he knew all the same. His nose started to run. A quick check found no handkerchief, not even a pocket. Only a rip, a thin line of waxed thread where the seam had been. His sister had promised to mend it and hadn't bothered. Good old Avril, dependable in a crisis. He sniffed hard, hoped for the best, and went inside.

Nothing yet, Mr Blair, the big shop woman said. She was wrapping a ration of butter for a customer, a skinny sort who tilted her eyes sideways at him from under a hat. Sometimes things take a wee while.

Oh dear. The hat lady looked over sympathetically.

Can't be helped, he said. He cleared his throat.

I'll have Davie bring the parcel up to Barnhill, when it comes, the shop woman said. Her arms were braced on the counter now, in charge. You'll catch your death coming and going.

I'm sturdier than I look, he said, hoping for lightness,

13

but the women exchanged a glance. They had the look of his sister, the pair of them, all motherly contempt. Most women, except the younger sort, did.

I'll try in a few days, he said. Thanks all the same.

Davie was a good enough chap, but he didn't want anyone else poking through his mail. A pistol was not a usual kind of delivery and it would cause comment. He was conspicuous enough already. Since there was gin, he took one bottle and didn't ask for lemons even as a joke. Rationing this long after the war wasn't funny.

Your sister's cold is better, I hope, the big one said, ringing up. And your wee boy – Richard, is it? Both women sighed. That was a nasty fall, eh?

Richard's fine, thank you, he said, irked. Not even the doctor was discreet here.

Glass, though, and stitches, the skinny one said. They're so vulnerable at that age. No idea of danger.

No, he said.

The bell rang behind him in the middle of their best wishes. One of them waved.

At least the rain had stopped. The sea was flat as shark skin now, cloud lifting over the islands. Deer lowing in the distance said the threat had not gone completely, however. Out here, it never did. His calves ached with cold from the drenching of drive down, every new twist on the track throwing up mud. Avril would pull faces when he got back, say he should never have gone out in that kind of weather, but to hell with it. He had been out all day up a ladder with the apple trees only yesterday, then spent the evening on the hill, shooting rabbits. He had made Richard carry them, blood dripping from their eyes and noses. It mattered that one's son should not be sentimental. The fate of the weak, after all, was to fall. Soon, they'd patch the barn roof and clear the garden ready for winter, sort out the rats in the loft. There was plenty to do. He had no desire to stop what his sister called *being a Boy Scout* to rest. It was all the doctors told him. *Rest.* They had no idea what they were asking.

A shift overhead made the rain on the panniers shimmer before the light dulled again, showing the rust. All over the frame like fungus. He had carried a scythe on his back at one time, even when he drove, and it had scored the bodywork so badly the tank looked fit to split in two. It was twenty-three miles to Barnhill. If the damn thing broke down again – well, it just better not. The engine took three short kicks to turn over. Revving high, startling a sheep on the grass verge, he started the long ride back.

Past Knockrome, the road widened out into lines of rolling heather, peat and boggy turf. At the crest of the hill, the sea reappeared with its scatter of islands. Clumps of reed broke through the middle of the road, breaking what tarmac remained into a double stream. He could drive only by keeping close to the ditch, under assault by puddles and potholes, cottage loaves of dung. Today, it was slippery with leaves into the bargain, but light showed in glimpses under the heavy cloud, and it seemed he might yet manage home before another downpour. By comparison to the journey down, this was relaxation. Rest. The doctor's word, every doctor's word, wherever he turned. *Rest.*

The last time he'd had to suffer it was at Mrs Nelson's, the day of Richard's accident. No one knew how it had happened, but the screams brought them running to find a broken chair, shattered glass and Richard, bleeding. And he'd carried him all the way from Barnhill to Mrs Nelson's, mile after sodden mile because she had the telephone, the boy bloody as a shot stag.

A cut to the forehead always bleeds heavily, Mrs Nelson had said. It'll not be as bad as it looks.

And soon enough the doctor had struggled up from Craighouse with his black bag and beetled into the bathroom to start stitching. Mrs Nelson had assisted, instructing *Mr Blair* wait outside like an expectant father. He heard muffled moans and sobs then out she had come with Richard in her arms, five puckery black lines on his brow like a name gouged into wood. The child's eyes were wet, but he had put his arms out to be taken and fallen asleep almost immediately against the familiar scent of his father's tweeds.

The doctor was in no hurry to converse. Not immediately. Eric offered him a cigarette.

I hear you've been out sailing, the doctor said, nodding.

I keep myself busy. Eric lit a match, not sure where the question was leading.

You do, the doctor said. Word gets round. He looked down on the seated man like Zeus from Olympus. Mr Blair, I feel I have to speak. I know how severe your condition is. Even if I hadn't heard, I can see for myself.

Eric stiffened. The boy didn't budge.

TB isn't impressed by pluck, the doctor said. You don't fight an illness like this by fighting it. I'm telling you this very earnestly, Mr Blair. Rest. You've a book to finish. Your publisher must be anxious even if you're not. They'd tell you the same as me, I'm sure. *Rest*.

And Eric had nodded, silently incensed as the doctor handed over a tube of antiseptic cream, already half-used. His nails were too clean.

The boy will be right as rain, he said. It's you that worries me.

Mrs Nelson couldn't meet his eye.

He had worked off his rage by digging peats the following day, and taken Richard along for the exercise. They had spied on plovers from the bushes then chased each other the last half-mile home. Illness was one thing: being an invalid was another. Looking back, he was sure the doctor meant well, but he was narrow. They all were. If things went on the way they were going, the war over but politics still septic wherever one looked, all Europe would be blown to smithereens before they knew it. The bomb had changed everything. He, at least, knew it. If the worst happened, he could hold on in a place like this, a place too remote to bomb. Here, in more senses than one, they were un-get-at-able. Doctor's advice and a so-called *routine procedure* had finished Eileen off before her time and left husband and son high and dry. He was all the boy had left, and whatever happened, he could hang on till Richard was thirteen, surely. Just one decade. That was all he asked.

By Tarbert, the dark of the forest turned to unexpected brightness. Across the bay, the sky was lifting as he watched from purple to lavender to blue. If the road had not been so pitted, he would have pulled in the clutch and freewheeled to the foot of the incline. It was glorious, this freshness after misery, the sea pale and calm. Sometimes, the island and its surprises made anything seem possible. Maybe – the thought occurred as the sun came out – maybe could find another wife. He was ill, granted, but otherwise dependable. If he finished the book, if it sold in anything like the numbers his publisher hoped, he might even be rich. Avril wouldn't like the idea one bit, but these days Avril didn't like much at all. He pictured Avril, his own sister, nodding agreement while the specialist pronounced him as good as dead (*Mr Orwell, you may have less than two years at this rate*); Avril insisting he use the pen-name to get better treatment (*Let's face it, Eric, nobody cares two hoots till they know you're the Famous George*). Well, whoever the world and his ruddy sister took him for, he wasn't giving up the ghost yet. He would finish the book, make some money, get the farm running. Now he thought of it, he'd write another will into the bargain. Avril would send Richard to some dreadful boarding school if she ended up with him. He needs more discipline, just the way you did. She'd do it out of spite. The motorbike was bouncing over shale now, shaking him down to his bones. She wasn't getting Richard. One way or another, he'd make damned sure.

The wind was in his eyes.

Eric never wept, not even for Eileen, but from time to time, his eyes watered. He rubbed them with his left cuff as the bike scudded on. Great walls of layered rock were rising on either side obscuring the fields. Then, as he began the climb out of the valley, a crack rang out, a sound like the sky opening. At the same moment, the bike slid sharply sideways, the engine revving wildly as he rolled his grip on the handlebars. He was aware of the ditch to his left, the solid rock veering far too close, the crack of gunfire again, again as something fluttered overhead. The machine cobbled as he struggled to regain control, lost. It was then, as the bike tipped past the point of stability, he saw a face. Long and greyish, watching from the bracken, its eyes steady. The engine cut sharply as the machine crashed down onto the heather, Eric drawing back by instinctive sleight. Barely upright, he focused on the bracken, then wheeled, checking afresh, the sound of his own heart dinning in his ears. Now, however, with the light shifted and his gaze still, he saw the face was nothing. Mere rock, a bare patch showing pale against the terracotta ferns. He keeled forward, breathed deep and coughed till he almost retched. Not a face, he told himself, choking. No assassin, no accuser. It was no one at all.

Miraculously, the gin was unbroken, the bike in no worse shape than before. No one, so far as he was aware, had seen his fall, except pheasants. Stupid birds with no survival instinct. Even so, people shot them. It seemed poor sport. Another burst of gunfire sounded; distant wings, flailing. He wiped his mouth. There was a tear in the cloth of his trousers near the knee, seeping slightly. Other than that, he was unscathed. He allowed his shoulders to drop, almost smiled. He was still here. He was, after a fashion, fine.

The bike started first kick. Ahead was the way to Ardlussa. Tonight, he thought, staring ahead, he'd take Richard out, hunt rats in the barn with hammers. Things would be better when the Luger came. Meanwhile, they'd manage. Ravens wheeled in a nearby field, cawing. He had his book to finish, the farm to attend to, his son to raise. There were, in the real world, no alternatives. He lifted his feet and descended, roaring, into the home stretch.

Evans Walk

KATHLEEN JAMIE

i
Atlantic to Atlantic, ocean to ocean
the path climbs
up through lush grasses

Cloudless sky. Moor silent
but for fly-buzz.
Relief of the Abhainn Bheag
splashing over pebbles.

ii
In its sliver of shade
I rest, conversing
with a huge erratic boulder

about raised beaches,
glaciers, the last ice-age . . .
It is slow to answer.

iii
The path guides me
up over moor to the watershed,
where begins a chain of four lochans
then a westward flowing river.

The Paps are forbidding high
bare scree. But ahead, a V
-shaped notch in the land
reveals blue Atlantic, distant isle of Colonsay.

iv
Waterfalls, and a slog
across a plain of head-high
boggy, fly-ridden bracken.
Just one warbler singing.

v
On the white, empty
sands at Glenbatrick
I collect exquisite
mother-of-pearl shells.

vi
The same path back –
up to the pretty lochan
whose surface is flashing
electric-blue: dragonflies.

Watershed again.
In the distance, the mainland –
the blue Sound of Jura
one white sail, passing.

Orwell on Jura

BERNARD CRICK

I asked one Donald Darrock, who had once worked the croft at Kinauchdrach near to Barnhill and was later postman and gillie, 'Was Eric Blair a friendly man?' On Jura he always went by his real name. 'Aye, a friendly man right enough, a kind man, a cup of tea or a dram and the kettle was always boiling.'

Well, tight and forbidding though Orwell could be, a postman who had come the five miles up the rough track beyond the end of the single-track road could not just be sent away from the doorstep, especially as Orwell's post was sometimes heavy and always included the weekly joint sent from Loch Tarbert on the mainland on Friday mornings and delivered in late afternoon. But Mr Darrock said that Mr Blair didn't like strangers, whether strong hikers or from yachts, just dropping in to see what it was really like at the end of the track on the bleak northern tip. 'What did you talk about?' 'Oh the kind of things that men talk about over a dram.' 'Such as?' 'Oh I cannot remember – you know, the weather and the prospects' [for the season].

At first I was inclined to accept that the islanders who had met him only did talk the time of day, so nothing worth remembering. But a conversation with Angus McKechnie gave me pause. 'They say that he didn't get on well with his sister.' 'Oh I would not know.' 'A rather forbidding woman they say.' 'Oh aye, so they do say.' 'I have heard that he did not welcome his sister descending to look after him and driving his young housekeeper out.' 'Well now, you know what they say, "two women in one kitchen".' 'A Canadian poet visited him, I forget his name [I didn't] whom she did not like at all and she drove him out, short notice, the middle of an afternoon.' 'No, Paul Potts you mean, a poor gentleman. It was in the middle of the night. I heard his footsteps on the road to Craighouse.' So too late I realised that the islanders had remarkable memories even for small things which could to them on the small island loom large; but they also had a strong protective discretion with strangers (especially a biographer, whom they must have thought of as little better than a journalist or a detective sergeant). They were protective of someone whom, in those days before easy tourism and holiday cottages, the two hundred and fifty inhabitants could regard as *almost* one of them because he seemed settled on the island and was working a patch of land however cack-handedly ('not always did he know what he was doing'). However, 'he seemed a kindly man and he kept himself to himself and interfered with no one', a great virtue to the islanders, doubtless comparing him with some of the lairds. But they firmly saw him as – two different informants used exactly the same words, as if the judgement had been mulled slowly over pipe and dram – 'a peculiar and kindly gentleman'. For this bohemian presence was plainly in social class terms – not just evaluatively a gentleman (as in 'real Highland gentleman' said of even a poor man) – but a Gentleman indeed.

Towards the end of the war and amid the unexpected huge success of *Animal Farm*, Orwell had been living in a flat in Canonbury. But he found that sudden fame and too many friends, of very diverse kinds, from drunken poets like Paul Potts to grandees like David Astor, the proprietor and editor of *The Observer*, added up to constant interruptions and distractions. By early 1946 he knew fairly clearly what he wanted to write, what became *Nineteen Eighty-Four* but was nearly called *The Last Man in Europe*. So he told some of his friends that he wanted get right out of London to somewhere, anywhere remote, if possible without a telephone and difficult enough of access from London to deter, certainly in immediate post-war travel conditions, all but the most warmly invited and most resolute friends. David Astor happened to suggest, serendipitously, Jura. The Astors had an estate in the middle of the island and David had often met the laird of the north of Jura, Margaret Fletcher (née Nelson) at her house at Ardlussa where the tarmac road ended twenty-five miles from the hotel at Craighouse where, back then, the steamers came in. Five miles up the track from Ardlussa was a small house, Barnhill, and two or three miles beyond that were two croft cottages at Kinauchdrach. She had some difficulty finding tenants. Barnhill could hardly pay as a farm. There were two fields, worked from Kinauchdrach, and a vegetable patch, so there was only the illusion – which Orwell embraced, as a past master of doing simple things the hard way – of self-sufficiency in fruit and vegetables. So a writer with, by then, some income was an ideal tenant for Maggie Fletcher. It was pure coincidence that her then husband, who died in 1960, his health destroyed in Japanese prisoner-of-war camps, had been before the war a teacher at Eton where Orwell had, a decade or more before, been an ironic and sardonic scholarship boy.

He made a reconnaissance to Jura for two weeks in September 1945, only moving into Barnhill in May the following year, albeit returning to London in October for the winter and to wind up his affairs in Canonbury. However on 29 December he set off for Jura 'to plant fruit trees' he said, but there were travel problems and he did not arrive until late on 1 January. Presumably he was heading for Hogmanay to see, on a new learning curve, the real Scotland; but tragically missed that one night of all nights. The stiff-upper-lipped Englishman made no such admission but the dates speak for themselves even to the most cautious of biographers.

By August 1946 Orwell had begun work on *Nineteen Eighty-Four*, tap tapping away on his old portable, usually in his small upstairs bedroom while his sister down below froze out unwanted visitors or kept invited guests at bay until the evening. A particularly unwelcome guest to Avril was Sally McEwan, a former secretary at *Tribune* where Orwell had been literary editor after leaving the BBC in the last years of the war. For Sally not merely brought a child with her and a cat, who shrieking and wailing fought for territory or chastity all night with the resident tom, but she was a strict vegetarian too. This raised problems in a kitchen whose staples were hare, rabbit, venison, herring and lobster, not to mention the weekly Sunday joint in the post from the mainland. Eric and Avril at least had in common traditional domestic routines. The only thing Sally and Avril found in common was dislike of the free-thinking, monologuing, fantasising Paul Potts. Perhaps together they conspired his expulsion from what to him was his friend's Eden.

Remote though it was, I had the feeling that some of

Orwell's friends or acquaintances took more literally than he really intended that well meant but often not wholly sincere English upper middle-class politeness, 'Must come up and see my new place sometime, you know.' But one set of visitors came whom he really welcomed: his nephew and two nieces, the children of his late sister Marjorie Dakin. Henry Dakin was a second lieutenant in the army on leave, Jane had just left the Women's Land Army and her teenage sister Lucy was still at school. The happy visit was nearly the end of them all. To make up for neglecting them while in the dogged heat of writing, Uncle Eric proposed an expedition together with his three-year-old adopted son Ricky (Richard) whom he had cared for since the death of his first and true wife, Eileen, back in 1945. They went to the other side of the island in a small boat with an outboard motor and picnicked. Jane and Avril walked back to get on with the hay-making on such a fine day. But on the way back it seems that Eric had misread the tide tables. Instead of skirting the Corryvreckan at ebb-tide, one of the fiercest whirlpools in the northern world, they were passing it near to full flood. They got caught in the eddies of one of its many peripheral minor whirlpools. They were tossed about so much that the outboard motor came off its moorings and fell in the sea. Eric, completely calm, suggested that Henry, as the stronger, took the oars. They were pitched onto a small island, but the boat capsized in the water with young Ricky in it. The toddler emerged in the arms of an unflappable Eric and they all waited on the rock until they attracted the attention of, as one can usually find in an apparently deserted Hebridean coastline, a solitary lobster fisherman. He got a rope to them across the swell and pulled them one by one into his boat. As they walked back into Barnhill Avril and Jane called out, 'What kept you so long?'

This near death of the author of *Animal Farm* was worth a garbled paragraph in the *Daily Express*. One of three phones then on the island must have buzzed through the one switchboard in the post office, manned by one 'Effie' who knew everyone's business. The paragraph did not mention young Ricky, so it sounded vaguely heroic rather than – as some might say – reckless and irresponsible of Orwell.

Some visitors were deterred. He had hoped that Sonia Brownell would visit him, with whom he had had a brief affair in 1945 and who was to marry him in his very last days. But Sonia was Chelsea, silk stockings and jade cigarette holders, not even of the sub-Bloomsbury of the pubs which were the only 'clubs' for many of Orwell's ordinary friends. So his travel hints would have been off-putting rather than helpful and enticing. Allow forty-eight hours and bring stout boots, gum boots, oil skins, he said, and to be sure to bring her food rations as well as a little flour and tea:

> I am afraid I am making all this sound very intimidating, but really it's easy enough and the house is quite comfortable. The room you would have is rather small but it looks out on the sea. By the time you get here I hope we'll have got hold of an engine for the boat and if we get decent weather we can go round to the completely uninhabited bays on the west side of the island . . . At one of them there is a cave where one can shelter and at another a shepherd's hut which is disused but quite lovable where one could even picnic for a day or two . . .

He had better luck with Celia Kirwan, Arthur Koestler's sister-in-law to whom he had proposed but had turned him down gracefully and acceptably with a sincere 'but we must remain good friends for ever'; and they did. At least as elegant and as sophisticated as Sonia, she indulged him as well as her curiosity with a visit despite:

> Don't bring more luggage than, say, a rucksack or a haversack, but on the other hand do bring a little flour if you can. We are nearly always short of bread and flour here since the rationing. You don't want many clothes so long as you have a raincoat and stout boots or shoes. Remember the boats sail on Mondays, Wednesdays and Fridays, and you have to leave Glasgow about 8 a.m.

Celia with a rucksack is almost as unimaginable as Sonia in boots.

I think he would have stayed in Jura, with occasional trips to London on publishing business and to see old friends who could not or would not travel, if it had not been for the sudden acceleration of his endemic tuberculosis. He became more and more interested in the life of the crofters, mistakenly but understandably thinking them typically Scottish, rather than a variant of the many diversities of Scottishness. Indeed he went somewhat over the top (or overboard, as it were, plunging into deep whirlpools), in one of the last columns he wrote in *Tribune*, as ever serious, provocative and comical, but like the great humanist and essayist he was, not always trying to change our minds, more trying to startle us into thought.

> Up to date the Scottish Nationalist movement seems to have gone almost unnoticed in England . . . You have an English

or anglicised upper class, and a Scottish working class which speaks with a markedly different accent, or even, part of the time, in a different language. This is a more dangerous kind of class division than any now existing in England. Given favourable circumstances it might develop in an ugly way, and the fact that there was a progressive Labour government in London might nor make much difference . . . I think we should pay more attention to the small but violent separatist movements which exist within our own island.

'Violent' is strange, even if deliberately provocative. Perhaps he had been reading too much Hugh MacDiarmid, as untypical, as eccentric but as interesting and stimulating as himself. But he was beginning to think about Scotland as Scotland, not just an address where he could write undisturbed, well – more or less undisturbed.

Some writers have foolishly thought that Jura was the death of him, and a wee bit deliberate too. This is of a piece with lazy routine Freudian belief that *Nineteen Eighty-Four* is a classic example of 'the death wish', rather than the last book the poor man happened to write before he happened to die, already in hospital making notes towards a new and more conventional novel. Two American authors have famously written of his 'mad and suicidal sojourn on Jura'. I called this isothermic fantasy. Jura is not Aberdeen. The Inner Hebrides lie in the Gulf Stream with a prevailing south-west wind, not the Arctic north-east wind of the east coast. Frost and snow are rare. Twenty miles down the sound from Jura in Gigha with its Achamore House Gardens are one the finest azalea, camellia and rhododendron collections in the British Isles.

Orwell's posthumous reputation has brought many visitors to Jura, at times some say more than is endurable.

The owners of Ardlussa rightly try to stop cars going up the track to Barnhill. Too often their tractor and their man had to pull them from the ditch. And the tenants of Barnhill rightly resent casual tourists. Indeed with four full biographies of Orwell – my own, Michael Sheldon's, Gordon Bowker's and D.J. Taylor's – there is nothing new to learn, and Richard Blair has built a new Barnhill across in Ardfern. Nothing really need draw visitors north of the bar in Craighouse where they should drink a dram in his immortal memory. And the old postman told me that the dram Mr Blair gave him was always a double. Where the hell did he get the whisky from in those hard times? In his day there was not even a distillery on the island, let alone such a one as now.

The gardener's shed

KATHLEEN JAMIE

Spiderwebs at the skylight.
Swallow droppings on the earth floor.
A bee meanders through the half open

stable-door. Out in the orchard
apples swell. Raspberries
redden against a stone wall;

roses mixed with drifts
of faded pink geraniums show
through an arch in the beech hedge.

Here rests his spade. A riddle
leans behind a pail. A pair of gloves,
work-weary, hang from a nail.

Superstition

ROMESH GUNESEKERA

Duncan unlocked his pair of secateurs and snipped another deadhead. The New Dawn had bloomed much earlier than he had expected. He had told Walter, at the pier, that the whole of the top terrace had run amok. Snap dragons popping before the lilies, azaleas fluttering after the foxgloves, the agapanthus shooting in every direction. 'I dread to think what will happen with the cannas this year.' His imported Lucifer and his Black Knight both looked weary. Walter had chuckled and waggled his head. That is what Walter always did: chuckle at something knocking around in his head and beam like a lighthouse without saying a word. Between them they hardly ever had a proper conversation – a dialogue – but it suited Duncan. He liked talking to Walter, as he did to his plants, because he valued the opportunity to follow a train of thought to its very end, without interruption, and discover what might grow unfettered in his mind.

This summer evening though, with the sun's long rays skimming the sea at the end of the garden, he went about his business deadheading, trimming, pruning, without issuing a word to plant, pebble or even midge. He was a large man, slow moving, with big strong hands. Each stem he clipped, he carefully collected and placed in a green garden sack. Every now and again he would place his big boot in the sack and crush the clippings down.

35

After he finished with the rose, he moved down to the fuchsia by the fence. He clipped back the bush with quiet determination, shaping it to the line of the small isles in the bay below and making room for his Nepalese bramble to creep out and twinkle under the bright scarlet lanterns. When he moved on to clear the berry patch, he saw Walter wobbling on his bike as he made his way up the farm track. At the gate, he dismounted and took off his cap. He was panting.

'Good evening, Walter. A hard climb?' He waved aside an agitated cloud of midges.

Walter waved back, knocking a few more away, still out of breath. He put his cap back on and swivelled it into its groove. A small rivulet of sweat trickled down the side of his face into his limp collar. He tugged at it. 'Somebody has come,' he spluttered.

'On the ferry?' It was not unusual; there were often visitors to the island to climb the gold peak, sniff the fabled peat or visit the famous walled Gardens, especially with the new Jura ferry in operation. The mainland was now only forty-five minutes away.

Walter slapped the back of his neck. 'Asking after you.'

Duncan put the secateurs in his pocket and took off his thick, red pruning gloves. In the quiet teeming air his breath whistled in and out of him. 'Did he seem . . . official?'

Duncan had recently written to his supervisor at the Roebuck Trust for extra funding to renovate an old stable he wanted to turn into a heritage museum of native flora. He expected a visit, for a night of island malt, before the decision was made.

Walter laughed from somewhere at the back of throat. 'A woman.'

'Asking what?'

Walter shrugged. 'Abigail sent for Alex to drive her over. She looks foreign. Very determined . . . Abigail thought you should be warned.'

Isabel Cupido from Funchal, on the island of Madeira, was a hardy traveller. She had abandoned the family wine trade for flowers and ran a business exporting anthuriums to hotel chains all over Europe. Duncan had met her at the Funchal Spring Festival, two years ago, where he had been lurking among the aspidistras making notes for his research project on the domestication of subtropical ornamental foliage: *Bedding the Exotic*.

Isabel had caught him moistening the tip of his pencil, a habit he had not been able to shake off despite the advent of mechanically propelled stay-sharp lead.

'You shouldn't do that,' she had said, in English, destroying the anonymity he thought he had.

He had wanted to reply in Portuguese, but his Berlitz phrases drifted out of reach, as they always did at moments of need.

'It will blacken your mouth,' she had laughed.

Duncan remembered his mother saying that he should endeavour to speak well because the words one utters are for ever written on one's tongue. She was a poet and dead for fifteen years, but her own uninscribed words often came back to him at disconcerting moments, like unexpected swallows, to tease his speechlessness. 'Shall we have a coffee?' he had blurted out.

Isabel was in her late thirties and had no problem

.t having coffee with strangers who displayed the
.d fetish with objects in their hands. In her business she
was often drinking with men who could not stop fiddling
with Blackberries, PDAs or pens, however charming she
tried to be. Pencils were rare and evoked an era of simpler
phallic symbols, which intrigued her.

'You like anthuriums, or you prefer a floribunda?' she
asked, getting straight to the point, when they had taken
their seats at the Golden Gate café.

He evaded the question by stirring inordinate amounts
of sugar into his coffee. 'Depends . . . every occasion has
its own flower.'

'Every emotion, you mean.' She added a heavy breath
for emphasis. 'Are you a horticulturist?'

'A late flowering mature student . . .' Their chatter he
had thought was inconsequential, and it surprised him
when he realised, in the evening, that they had embarked
on an affair of heady passion. She was leggy, like her
anthuriums, and had an eager oval face; he had a burly
masculinity that among the pansies and the carnations
made him huggable. On the balcony of his room at the
Pestana she had gently bitten his fingers and said, 'The
mature horticulturist must dig deep, no, to grow the true
bloom of love?'

The next day, at the stall behind the perennials tent,
she had bought him a packet of seeds of the iconic bird
of paradise and a couple of agapanthus plants to take
home. 'Soak the seeds first, then plenty of mulch or good
chopped peat. You will think of me when they begin to
flower,' she joked.

He promised Isabel that he would return before the
twelfth of August, but once back at college he found

himself so immersed in exams and project work that she
like the espado and the chilled Madeira, faded into the
wistful wastes of an escapade abroad. They spoke a few
times on the telephone as she flitted from Warsaw to
Budapest selling anthuriums to brash new entrepreneurs,
but the pauses in their conversations became increasingly difficult to fill. When he had lost his mobile, and
with it her number, on the bus to the Paisley midsummer
conference on Peat and Climate Change in the Hebrides,
it was something of a relief. He realised he liked things
to stay where they are planted, whatever happens to the
ionosphere.

'How did you find me?' he asked her when she turned up
at the gate. This was an island famous for its unget-at-
able remoteness, at least until the new ferry had started.

'Are you not pleased to see me?' Isabel kept her hands
in her pockets.

'You've changed your hair.' She had it short at the back
and high on top, with one bleached blonde streak parting
the black. Her eyebrows were thicker and had straight-
ened into a sharp dangerous cliff.

'You stopped calling.' Her teeth clicked after the accu-
sation.

'I lost my phone. All my numbers. It seemed like fate,
after our last few calls.'

'You believe in providence, do you?'

A small knot in his stomach made him wince. When he
first arrived on this Hebridean isle, he had been told the
tragic tale of the gardener at the Lodge who had trans-
gressed the customs of the island and defied providence.
The man had become infatuated with a raven-haired

oman who lived in a pauper's cottage at the edge of the village. A wild woman who fashioned her clothes out of old flour bags and meal sacks. She had asked him to make a raised lazy-bed of seaweed for her cucumbers and carrots. He had obliged and tended her vegetables assiduously but could not get her plants to thrive. Nevertheless, for his endeavours she rewarded him with oxtail soup and a peat bath, laced with whin and elderberries, where she massaged his feet and gave him gratification he had never known before. One cold April, she had asked him to cut more peat from the hills as her stack was low. He had protested; it was against the wisdom of the island to cut peat before May. She had scoffed at him. You go by old wives' tales, like a wee mouse, do you? Can you not satisfy the desires of a natural woman? Will you spurn my hot bath in the spring? Against his better judgement he did as she had asked, and provoked the wrath of the disturbed land. She died from a poisoned prick while picking belladonna berries that summer, and was found with child. He was distraught. He stopped pruning and walked the beaches kicking at seaweed and clumps of bedraggled camomile. He lost his job, his stone house and eventually the grip of his mind. He died penniless in the ramshackle pauper's cottage with wild fuchsia breaking through the roof, and hydrangea obscuring the windows, railing at the monkshood, the phantoms of his ill luck and wet peat.

'I couldn't find you. I looked on the Internet, there was no link.'

'I went to the Golden Gate every Saturday for months. All you had to do was come to Funchal and walk in.'

He remembered the café: how he had moistened his pencil to write down her number on a flyer for sea safaris on that first day. She had laughed and said, 'You don't need to write it. I'll call you and then my number will be on your phone.' She had done it straightaway, and he had put away his pencil and done it back to her.

'I am sorry I couldn't get away.'

'Did not, ever again.'

'By the time . . . autumn just seemed too late.'

'Too late? What, you thought I had wilted and died?'

He realised then that he did not know what he had thought, except that things thrived only when *all* the conditions were right. 'You were very busy.'

'The business folded.'

'I am sorry.'

Isabel shut her eyes and took a deep breath. 'I was pregnant.'

The agapanthus next to the buddleia wavered; their long stems were not as erect as those along the levadas of Madeira. The fretted purple globes of bloom were smaller, stayed lower. The hosta were turning blue while the hydrangea struggled to unfurl. The pressure in his chest made Duncan sway a little. He was trying to think of what to say but nothing in his head would stay in place. The buddleia had bees swarming all over it. The creamy New Dawn rose climber, which had flowered profusely, seemed to sag towards the ground. 'A child?'

'The pregnancy lasted five and a half months. It changed my life.'

'No child?' His thoughts collided going both ways on one track.

Isabel spotted the agapanthus. 'Are those the ones I gave you?'

'We have a micro-climate and plenty of good peat.'

He grasped for the facts. A good horticulturist must make the conditions right; tend, care, look after. 'You can grow almost anything here, with a bit of luck.'

'Even a late flowering Madeiran . . . ?'

Duncan stared at her sharp eager face and remembered the heady exuberance of their first spring. The true bloom. His mother once wrote, *what blossoms in the mind, like in the womb, is rooted in your heart.* 'I believe so,' he said. 'As long as you don't cut the peat before May.'

Cornucopia

LIZ LOCHHEAD

Darling, it is your birthday.
This would be the twentieth we have woken up to
    together
– except last year you were in hospital
and I woke alone at home early in our empty wide bed
thinking of you a mile away in that
bleak narrow one with the hospital corners.

Today I woke first – the sun so bright it almost hurt
streaming in through that swathe of
white linen at the window
and, picture of health, your head on the pillow
ablaze in its storm of grey curls I love.
Caught the sun, caught the sun, my love,
didn't you, yesterday
on our first full day on the Isle of Jura?

Was it late in the afternoon, exposed on that
clifftop walk we took from above the Ferry at Feolin
past Sailor's Grave towards Inver and
the ruins of Cnocbreac?
Was it earlier in the deceptively dappled light
on the walk to Jura House Garden?
On the shore path at Ardfin, where the
fuschia flared and the flagrant rhododendrons blossomed

along the loud banks of the Abhuinn Beag Burn?
Was it when we took our picnic of
oatcakes and cheese and apple and lay in the sun
against the rocks at Traigh Ban, the White Beach
remember? Where those five blond tall
teenage lads, down from the Big House, no doubt,
were splashing and shouting in the surf till they
ran out, shaking themselves like dogs, laughing,
then paused to pass a pleasant time of day with such
impeccable public school good manners
it was almost parodic?
Was it when, alone again on the empty beach,
we squinted into the sun
and looked for Heather Island and the ruined castle,
argued whether in the distance
what we could see was Arran, Kintyre or Ireland –
and you were trying to persuade me, teasing that
it might just be worth it to brave the water's cold?
Did we catch too much sun later
in the blaze of the gardens,
among the astonishing arches, barbered slopes
and walled gardens of exuberant exotica?
Was it when I lingered in the shade of the sheds
selecting us each an artichoke for supper,
till, leaving the money in the trustbox,
I came out into the sun again to
see you with Peter Cool the gardener,
who was showing you, cupped in his hand, that
perfect-looking house martin that somehow could not fly?
No, I think we burned up
as we drew by the tea tent,
you and I facing in different directions,

so engrossed in what we were doing
we didn't notice time passing or the sun beating down
or those so cheeky chaffinches sneaking under
the paper napkins to steal our lemon cake.
Yes, we must have spent an hour, more,
you with your big blue A3 sketchbook, I with my green.
Your choice (outward) was wildmeadow, trees, sky, sea
mine, didn't know why, simply the tea tent.
Was it that in my mind sang out the first line
of the sonnet *she is as in a field a silken tent?*
Was it the cool dark of its interior, taut ropes,
the festive arabesques of its tent-white roof
against the intricate sky?
The swipe of its bonny blue awning?
Was it my longing to
loop across the page with blue those scalloped edges
and dot the tall swathes of long grass and wildflower
with poppies, kingcups, dandelions and something blue?
I remember when it was time to pack up you said:
OK, a challenge, five minutes, we change sides
and draw the other person's view and,
as it happened,
in five minutes
you caught more than I had in that whole hour.
Wake up, my twenty years' love, and see
how many things can happen today . . .

That whisky we had a nip of last night had already
made it to its bourbon cask for ageing
when your Dionysus curls were black as grapes
and I buried my face in them on the
first

of the lovely,
finite
birthdays we'll have together.

Wake up, wake up
in this ridiculous room with the huge shell
bigger than a basin on the chest of drawers
for this is a house of many concetti
and here where we sleep
the motifs
are the coral and the scallop and the conch,
a mollusc multitude
of small shells that are cockles whorls and spirals
tiny dishes of mother of pearl and unicorn horns all
spilling from the ceiling's chandelier
like grapes from a cornucopia.
So wake up, won't you,
and enjoy being us
inside the shell of this morning
here in the White Room?
In the bleached light, the
only colour
your old blue tee-shirt over the back of the basket chair
and the mottled, bottled shells
in those glass jars beside that great pile of blue-grey,
slate-grey, sea-washed pebbles
making a raised beach of the mantelpiece.

The big deep roll-top bath that stands in this bedroom
is the biggest and shiniest shell of all,
its inside so new it's nacreous.
Oh, I'm going to let the

Buck's Fizz we always have on birthday breakfasts
spill over
as I lie up to my neck in bubbles,
swigging it, be the
oldest, plumpest, homeliest, happiest,
most shameless Aphrodite on the half shell –
white curtains wide open
to the astonishing un-Scottish sun and the dazzling sea
and you, my love,
sprawled across the bed opposite
talking to me and opening your presents.

Word in your shell-like, sweetheart,
wake up!
With your birthday
a whole day
a holiday
before us.

Shadows

SWETHA PRAKASH

And here is love, Chandika thinks. In monophor
togetherness, two corncrakes consort on the shingle
beach, swaying to their own music. She sketches quickly:
the ecstatic birds and the rugged coastline. It hasn't
rained today and she has been out for almost five hours,
sketching on her Moleskine pad. She knows the island
well now. Mostly uninhabited, its archaic wildness is at
once elevating and frightening. 'Landscape and Fear',
Chandika thinks, another possible theme.

Over a month on the island and Chandika has still
not found the focus for her art, its fulcrum and core.
During the day, she explores the heather-covered island,
taking visual notes on its peat hills, naturally formed bays,
scree-laden quartzite mountains, wooded coastlines and
dense kelp forests. At night, she paints. But her work so
far has been languid, like a dull migraine. It doesn't have
a real voice, a live presence she could talk to, quarrel and
agree with. She hasn't been able to capture the energy, the
vitality of the island. Its essence.

The island is in bloom. Its peat moors are covered with
heather, patches of bracken and deer grass sedges. Along
the coast, knotted and serrated wracks colonise the rocks
in horizontal bands. The shore is fringed with oarweeds,
carrageen and sea lettuce. Barnacle geese arrive in long
V-shaped skeins from their Greenland breeding grounds

to settle on the tidal flats at the head of the lochs. It is so complete and full in its ripeness that all artistic efforts to comment on it seem futile. The island assaults her senses with its beauty and primitive abundance. This fecund vegetation, this all pervasive fertility, seems to taunt Chandika about her present barrenness, her inability to create.

As she sketches the corncrakes, immersed in their playful lyrical symphony, Chandika thinks of Ram. Of the days when they used to work in creative harmony. Her art-school friends had been surprised when she started collaborating with him. *With a photographer? There is no art to photography, you just take a camera and click, anyone can do it. How can you create with someone else? Art only germinates in solitude.*

Chandika had always punctuated her paintings with other media – newspaper reports, poems, posters. With Ram, she started creating art installations that juxtaposed found objects, her paintings and his photographs on the same theme. They would play with space to create an intense sensory and narrative experience for the audience.

They complemented each other. For Chandika, the starting point was *bhava*, the inexpressible inner dream-world from which the outer world later emerged, while Ram immersed himself in the visible world, opening himself to any meaning it might offer. When Chandika was young, her parents would take her to *jugalbandi* concerts – where traditional dhoti-clad Indian carnatic musicians would perform in sync with western jazz musicians, in a spontaneous fusion of styles. Working with Ram was an artistic *jugalbandi*, a well coordinated ballroom dance. They presented different versions of the same story; their work was visually tied with a single spirit, a sustained rhythm. Was.

This is their last project together – to create an art installation inspired by Isle of Kreem for the local hotel here. They can't get out of the assignment. Once it is done, they will be free. Disentangled. If it gets done, Chandika thinks. Their break-up has drained her. How can you create when the only *bhava* you feel is emptiness?

And here, a close-up of a harbour seal on a grey cragged rock. It is posing for Ram: tilting its short muzzle towards him and twisting its rounded, spindle-shaped body. The light is overhead and harsh; the umbral shadow of a rough crag falls on the mottled body of the seal. Inhaling deeply, Ram holds his breath. He is shutting out the distracting sounds that envelop him – the steady hushing of the waves, the screeching choughs and the clambering wind. He concentrates on the composition, edits the visual frame till he is satisfied that all the narrative elements are just right. Ram looks for mortality and fragility in his subject. For him, photography serves only one purpose – to find beauty in the debris of a fleeting moment.

Ram has spent most of the day at Ealachan Bay, meditating on the vowels and consonants of the landscape. He wants the syllables of the island, its hushed inner truth to seep into his limbs. His photography teacher Krishnan used to say, 'Every landscape has an unmanifest character that can only be experienced when you submerge yourself in it. When you become one with it.'

The island exasperates and exhausts Ram with its vastness. Peat and rainwater have withered his walking boots and he constantly worries about his equipment.

The island, shaped and sculpted by the last ice age, is wild and largely inaccessible. It is stylish, constantly moving. Ram likes photographing the island after it has been rain-tossed, when the varicose-lined earth swells revealing her secret operas and cantatas.

Ram had dreaded coming here. Spending three months with Chandika, on a remote island, so soon after their turbulent split. But they hardly ever meet, having agreed to work independently on their respective productions for the installation.

The heartbeat of this severe, elegant island has revived him, acting like the mythical healing herb – the *sanjeevani bhooti*, reminding him that the world is still alive, that life goes on despite combustible relationships.

The portrait of the seal done, Ram walks on. He navigates through sand dunes held up by marram grass and rocky outcrops. He is looking for shadows – sharp, deep, striking. The sky darkens like undeveloped film. Ram smiles.

And here is a surprise – the smell of tree roots in a shingle beach. The wind, like an old Gaelic song, swishes and swirls around Chandika. She is looking at the sea, which is skimmed-milk white in the morning light. She holds a scallop shell in her hand. It is closed with mud inside. Reveal yourself, she whispers to it and puts it against her cheek. Dread, like the aftertaste of a paracetamol, is stuck in her throat.

She has never had artist's block before. Art has never been painful, a must-do chore like laundry-and-dish-washing. Her earliest memories are related to art. When Chandika was seven, she accidently stepped on a lizard while playing *stapoo* with her neighbours. After that, she had recurring nightmares about large Himalayan lizards chasing her down school corridors. To ward off these persistent imaginary lizards, Chandika stopped sleeping. She would stay awake by copying pictures from her illustrated storybooks into her notebooks. Soon, Chandika was not satisfied with merely copying other people's pictures, she wanted to make her own. She started keeping a visual dairy, drawing her desires, yearnings and impressions left over from the day. In school, she was consistently sent out of class for doodling in her textbooks and notebooks. She spent her library hours reading artists' biographies. Her first proper painting, on canvas, was a pastiche of Picasso's paintings – 'Dora Maar au Chat', 'Guernica' and 'The Old Guitarist'. During adolescence, that period mandated for crushes and infatuations, she gloriously declared to her aghast friends that Picasso was the love of her life and that she would never consider any school-going substitute.

She made the natural progression – enrolling in an art school. However, the classical training she received bored her. They were instructed to practise and practise and practise till they arrived at something that looked graceful and effortless. For Chandika, the conception, gestation and accouchement of her art had to be spontaneous, intuitive, drawn from the underground, unseen sea of her dreams.

That space inside her seems to have dried up now. All she carries with her is the memory of the relationship that disintegrated in a few hours, the layered insults, the rage.

At the edge of her mind, clenched like a fist, Chandika feels the desire to flee, to leave the island. What if she can't finish the project in time, conceive the art she wants?

Dream up images, that come from her bones. Sharp art: tastily made, well-shaped.

And here, beside the wind-chiselled coastline, a shell mound in leaf-filtered light. Intense and aquamarine, the sky sparkles. To maximise the field of view, Ram moves back. He spent the morning tracking the ever changing mountain light on the Beinn an Bo, a mountain largely composed of scree and large lumps of quartzite. A dull choir of pain is now lodged in his leg, but Ram doesn't want to return to the hotel. Ram despairs that he has only two more months on the island and he doesn't want to waste any time indoors.

It is a soundless day, serene and memory-stirring. Ram thinks of that aperture in his life when he first resolved to become a photographer. This reminiscence begins with a video shop. Ram was twelve when his family bought their first VCR. Every Friday, Ram and his brother Shyam were allowed to go the local video store and pick movies which they could watch over the weekend. He had found the new world – technicolour Hollywood with its smashing heroes, grand heroines, heated dialogues and stunning locales. After that, night after night, he had the same dreams – of either becoming a Clint Eastwood-style hero (constantly on the move) or a Bond villain (who, it must be admitted, made far-sighted exploration plans). After school, in the time allocated for homework, Ram would have imaginary conversations with Marco Polo, Sir Francis Drake and Captain Cook. In time, he discovered that photographers are the closest 'real world' descendents of the early travellers. Ram built his first darkroom, in their house's basement, when he was fifteen.

Years later, he first met Chandika in another darkroom. In those pre-digital camera days, he used to rent a darkroom in a photo studio on Narasimha Street. Chandika came into the studio, with the abstracted air of someone who had walked out of a Man Ray portrait, and asked for any spare chromogenic film they might have. She was collecting found objects for her next collage.

They met again, a year later, in an advertising agency. Ram had just quit his job as the staff photographer at *Hindusthan Today*, a monthly news magazine. He had been working with the magazine for four years, travelling around India doing photo-features. The travel was always stirring and satiating, but he had constant disagreements with the editors on the type of photographs he should be taking. He was asked to manipulate situations to get sensational and dramatic photographs (*We need to keep up with the competition, machaan, no one will pick up the magazine if we don't add some spice, some masala*). This corruption disturbed him. Ram was often angered by the way his photographs were selected and presented by the magazine. No amount of complaining helped, so he left. This, for Ram, was the beginning of a new life, a life woven with dreamscapes and days that smelt of turpentine.

He had started freelancing in the same advertising agency as Chandika. They discovered a mutual love for cityscapes. Chandika delighted in reconstructing the overcrowded city – rushing, panting and marinating in its own misery. Her paintings were dense; tale-like, infused with symbols. Layered, scarred.

Sharing the same energy levels, their discussions, like the ploughing of fields, were always lively and productive.

They were both interested in space and how audiences experienced space. They started creating site-specific art, arranged with an ensemble of objects, art and photographs that worked together to create a whole. Art like a chant, full and satisfying. Complete in itself.

She was also one of his favourite subjects. He would make little homemade books on *khadi* paper filled with her portraits – early morning Chandika in grey dungarees and a sweatshirt looking wide-eyed and slightly fuddled, Chandika painting with her fists and elbows, Chandika in a green towelling dressing gown earnestly studying herself in the mirror.

Nostalgia and remorse circles and builds in him, like a deepening scale of musical notes. He remembers her arms, safe like a life jacket. He regrets the hot spurt of anger that caused their break-up.

Overhead, the light caramelises, reminding Ram that he should be working. He changes the lens. He wants to photograph flat periwinkles perched on toothed wrack fronds: the macrocosm hidden in the microcosm.

Their last project. The City Council wanted them to do an installation on 'Sleep and the City' in Bangalore's biggest space – the Chowdiah Hall. They were also asked to organise a huge inauguration event inviting the who's who of the city. For six months, they imagined and fashioned the installation.

They were artists, not event managers. Neither of them paid attention to mics, projectors, podiums, invitations. Small things like that. They just presumed that if they took care of the art – the photographs, the paintings, the creative space, the rest would manage itself. But it didn't. The event was a disaster. The sponsors screamed at them and they got terrible reviews. Disgrace, so much disgrace, public disgrace.

Afterwards, when they were alone with their failure, Ram said, 'It's your fault.'

A bitter lining of disbelief coated Chandika's tongue. How could he blame her alone for what had happened? A small void opened up inside her: anger like a blooming flower. They fought, for hours.

This room, like hers, is coral pink. It has the musty smell of antiquated, yellow books. The sliding sash window opens to a machair view. She enters the room hesitantly, inhaling a long calm-down breath. Her face is tight and polite. They haven't spoken since they came to the island. When they meet in the hotel's communal areas, the mutual acknowledgement is clumsy, brief.

Ram is wearing a beige Fab India kurta and taupe jeans. He smiles, his russet eyes clear as a burn, 'Thanks for coming. How are you?'

'Good, you?' Chandika sits on antique cigar leather sofa. Here it comes, she thinks, he is going to ask me about the installation. Chandika decides that she will lie; she doesn't want him to know about her block. Disquiet, like a terrier, is leaping in her chest. She regrets that she agreed to meet him.

Ram sits on the white linen château chair; his hands locked, as if in self protection.

And now, the silence of an intensive care ward; dots and dashes of embarrassed silence, patterned like a formal dance.

Ram speaks, his voice tidy and slow.

It takes Chandika a few minutes to understand the shape of his words, to realise that this is an apology.

An apology, stacked up like vertebrae.

When Chandika returns to her room, the taste of bitterness, coiled within her like a serpent since the fight, disappears. There is a feeling gathering inside her; like an inner rain, it fills her. She shuts her eyes and when she opens them time seems to restart. The theme, yes, she knows it now – the island, fluidly swaying to its own rhythm, its well-timed dance. Chandika smiles; she is back in the womb, in the place where absences are given life and shape.

DIH-RAH

oak gall landscapes

Stage 1: outward
Kennacraig-Islay-Jura

David Faithfull

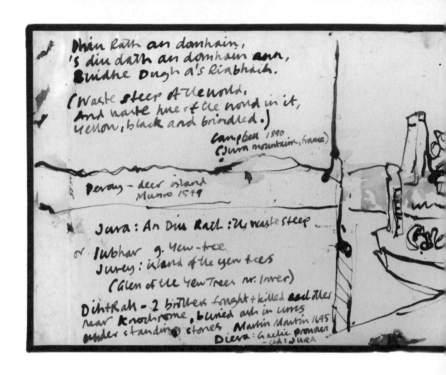

A

Oak gall ink drawings and palindromic landscape studies by David Faithfull giving an uninterrupted record of the entire ferry journey to and from Jura in September 2008, while travelling to collaborate with the writer and poet John Burnside on the island.

An accompanying limited edition Artist's Book has been produced for the Isle of Jura Distillery and the Scottish Book Trust incorporating these images together with John's poems.

Ferry at Kennacraig

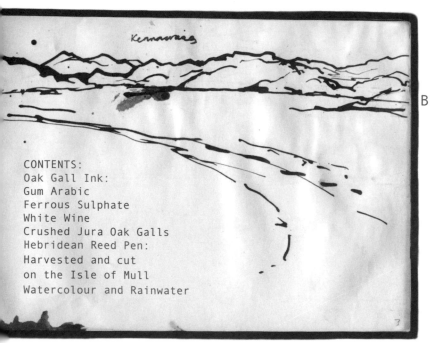

CONTENTS:
Oak Gall Ink:
Gum Arabic
Ferrous Sulphate
White Wine
Crushed Jura Oak Galls
Hebridean Reed Pen:
Harvested and cut
on the Isle of Mull
Watercolour and Rainwater

Panoramic seascape A-B (Kennacraig-W.Loch Tarbert)

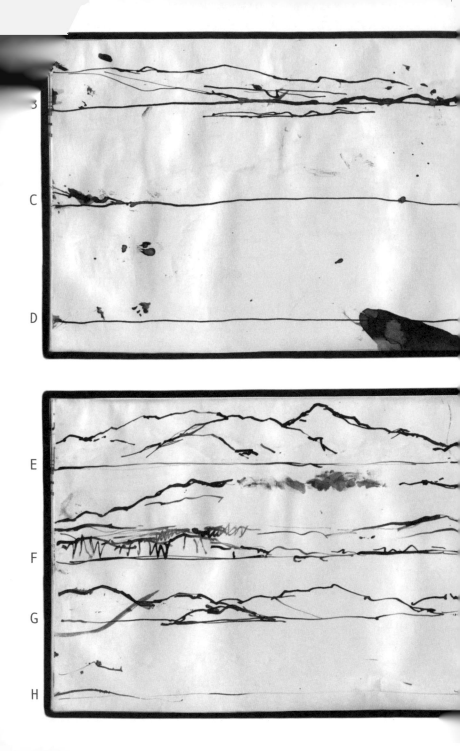

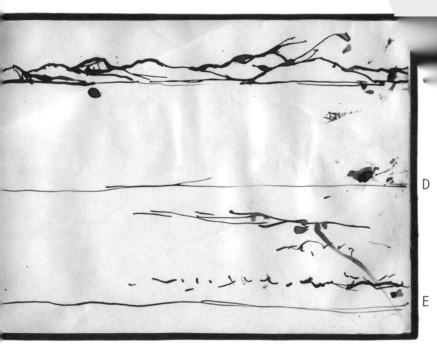

D

E

Panoramic seascape B-E (Kintyre-Gigha-Islay)

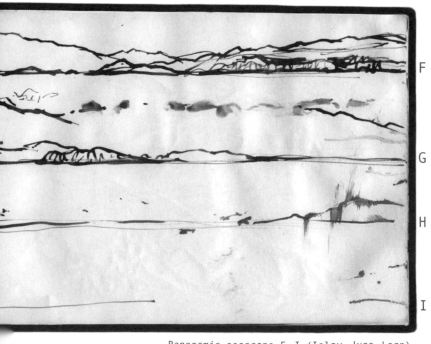

F

G

H

I

Panoramic seascape E-I (Islay-Jura-Lorn)

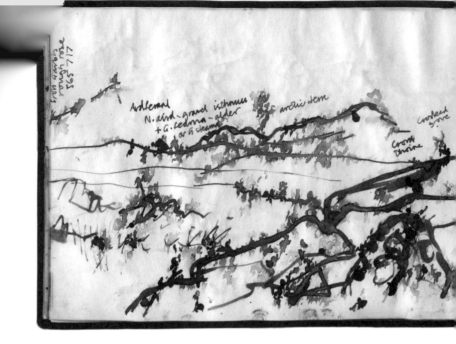

Ashlemal
N. dird-grand isthmus
+ G. Ledma-alder
. or G. steamp?

arctic tern

Crooked grove

Cronk
Divine

522658

Craigais Hill
N. krak-
crow + v
hark

527670
craighouse

My

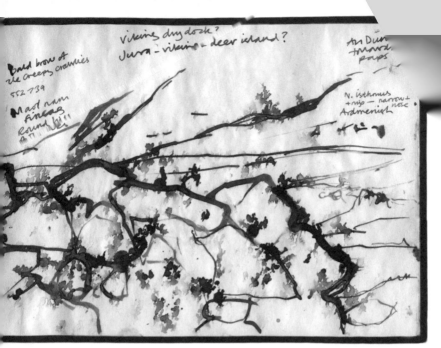

viking dry dock?
Jura – viking – deer island?

bald brow of
the creepy crannies

552 739

Maol nam
finea[?]
Round [?]

An Dun[?]
toward
paps

N. isthmus
+ mjo – narrow +
Ardmenish
nose

Paps from An Dunan

524654
Dunan Ubha
(cairdonure (cairn)

[2 hooded crows
on tree stumps.]

Sannaig
N. sand +
vik – harbor

Crackaig Hill

Beinn Shiantaidh
513747
757m
peak of
the storms

— Corra Bheinn —
525756
—573m
steep peak

Leac Fhola
Slab of blood
559773

814m

Corra
Bheinn from
Evans Walk

Leac
Fhola

from Loch na Cloiche
Loch of the Stone
539757

10

Beinn Shiantaidh and Leac Fhola

Evans W...

15

Paps and Evans Walk

J

K

K

Panoramic seascape J-K (Jura)

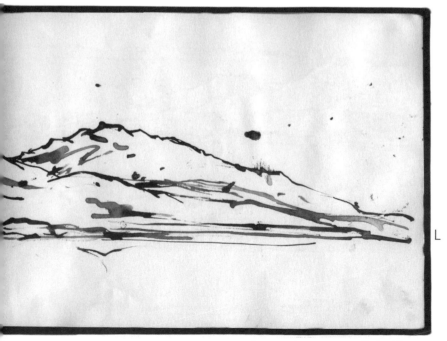

L

Panoramic seascape K-L (Jura)

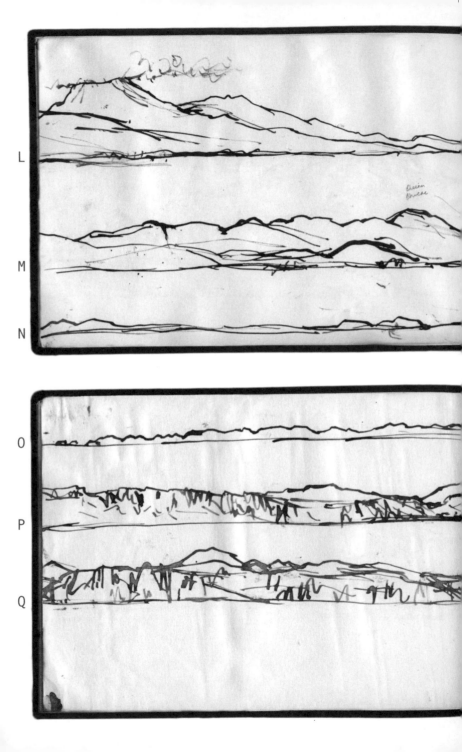

L

M

N

O

P

Q

Panoramic seascape L-O (Jura-Islay-Colonsay)

Panoramic seascape O-R (Mull-Lismore)

Notes

Palindromic Landscape: from 'Palindromos' (Greek) 'Running back again'

An Diu Rath: (Gaelic) 'the waste steep'
(J.F.Campbell *Popular Tales of the West Highlands* 1890)

Dih and Rah: '...two brethren, who are believed to have been Danes...Tradition
says that these two fought and killed one another in the village Knock-Cronm,
(Knochrome: the bowed hill) where there are two stones erected of 7 feet high
each, and under them, they say, there are urns, with the ashes of the two
brothers...'
(Martin Martin *A Description of the Western Islands of Scotland* 1695)

Diurath or Diera (combination of Dih and Rah) - pronounced in Gaelic as 'Jura'.
(G. Wright *Jura's Heritage* 1994)

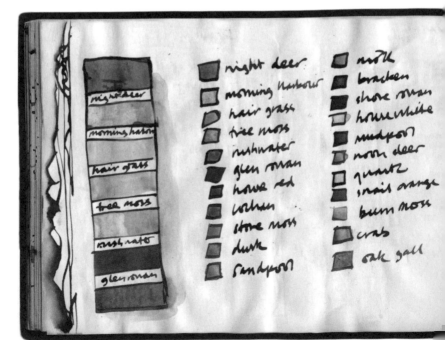

The oak galls used in these drawings were collected by David Faithfull on a reconnaissance trip to Jura in August 2008.

Iron gall or oak gall ink was revered by calligraphers and artists for centuries and was used by the Celtic monks illuminating the pages of The Book of Kells around 800 AD, possibly scribed on the nearby Island of Iona.

As part of the collaborative process, a Hebridean reed pen and a phial of the ink made from the Jura galls (following an old medieval recipe) were sent by David to John Burnside, during his residency at the Jura Distillery Lodge, in September 2008.

Jura and Scarba from Mull

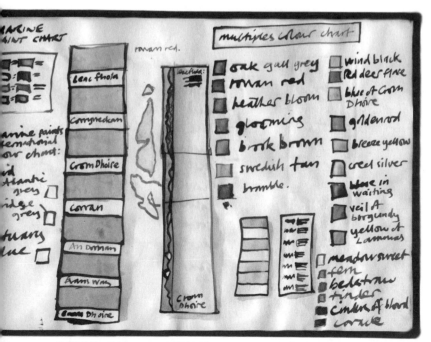

Colour palette reflecting John Burnside's Jura poems

AN DIU RATH

palindromic landscapes

Stage 2: inward
Jura-Islay-Colonsay-Oban

Semper Fidelis

Deer Island

JOHN BURNSIDE

The old days were better for mourning;
better for tongue-tacked girls in ruined plaid
climbing a hillside to gather the rainwashed bones
of what they had lost, that winter, to the cold;

and men in the prime of their lives, with dwindled sight,
gathering rowans to lay on an empty grave
and thinking of the dead, away at sea,
who dream of nothing more than Leac Fhola

− and to think they are always here
in the near blossom

waiting to be propped
in blood and bone

and finding the nub of a voice
with which to name

the hairline in the grass
where something falls

and quickens: flames
of meadowsweet and fern

and Lady's bedstraw
streaming in the dark.

The isle is full of noises:
river-run, culvert, boot-plash, passing storm,

– and those whisperers out on the ledge
in a black wind,

come to a murmur, then gone
in the turn of the tide;

a red deer flares from the verge
in the headlamps' glamour

and something we cannot name
returns from the dark

away to the side somewhere,
or behind our backs,

running across the sands
with printless foot

and vanishing into the blue
of Cróm Dhoire

Now that they are meadowsweet and thyme

and sand bees drift through their veins
from Knockrome to Corran

the children go back and forth, in the wind-coloured
   shadows,
gathering brambles; brushing the lips of the dead.

– and to think they are always here
in the near blossom,

drifting in their hundreds through a stand
of goldenrod, behind an abattoir:

cinders of blood and fur
in a yellowing breeze,

they always looked like this,
had you but known,

like fingertips in abstract
or a child's

refusal to come in
out of the sun,

and always a recognition of their kind
in everything we use and set aside:

forceps; reed pen; fishnet; coracle;
shroud pin; cleaver; bone saw; gutting knife.

Tell me again how the dead will return from the dark

and every track that cuts across the moor,
every door left open to the night,

every boat and creel left on the shore
will silver with the memory of waiting.

I miss them so well, I could almost believe they are here,
– be not afeard, the isle is full of noises –

they fall to a murmur
then blossom in waves on my skin,

one, and by one, back to the steadfast earth
beloved and piecemeal, in coffers of hairsbreadth and bone.

A night for the lesser
familiars:

the saddle cut's blue-in-waiting,
the harboured boats

*– eau de nil, storm grey,
signal green, ocean blue –*

the wind in the slats
of the larder, folding the skinned

carcass
in a veil of burgundy

and out at the end of the track:
the rowan, in its sleeve of tattered moon,

where, once, in the yellow of Lammas,
you buried a heart

and waited,
through the tenderness of snow,

for antler buds
or flakes of edelweiss.

See, they return
                    – the louche dead, blown through the gaps
in roofbeams, or the smoored ash of a fire:

bee-drift and sand-drift, struck from the lamplit chill
of fuchsia, at the near edge of the world,

or something in the air, above An Dúnan,
tipping against the wind, then coming true

– the isle is full of noises
                    one, and by one –
the slimmest of chances, the instance, the harrier soul.

Enough

PHILIP GOUREVITCH

This was what he did when he felt like a failure: he withdrew. Erika said he withdrew into himself. He said, No – his self was no refuge. He understood what she meant, of course, the figure of speech. But when he felt like a failure he could not accept that anyone might understand him. That would contradict his despair. He did not want to see anyone and he did not want to be seen and so he made himself unsightly: he drank a great deal and slept very little and gave up on grooming and laundry. He did not want to talk to anyone, so he spoke only when he felt he had to, and the speech came in brief bitter outbursts that surprised him and gave him no relief.

He said things like, 'No, no – don't console me. Don't even try. It is pointless. Don't dare. Please, don't patronise. You cannot understand. You cannot relate. You will only make it worse. Your consolation is anathema to me. Don't protest. This has nothing to do with you. I'm sure your consolation is excellent, and your sincerity first-rate. I just don't want it – not yours, not anybody's. Isn't that obvious? Is it so outrageous to be inconsolable? Is it such an affront? Does my affliction afflict you? Please don't forgive me. I make no apologies. And I blame nobody. I have nobody but myself to blame. Do you hear me? Nobody but myself. I know this makes me intolerable. Please don't tolerate me.'

Talking really was useless. So he withdrew further into his private squalor, the black mood that had its reasons but quickly grew beyond them to become its own all-encompassing unreason.

There were times when feeling that bad could feel pretty good. He didn't deny the perverse tremors of pleasure that came from wallowing in the murk of his soul, with language running riot in his head, until the din of his own flailing being drowned out the wars that were his livelihood. That's what he had done with his years: he went to the wars, and he went through them, and he wrote about them, and he got praised for it, because he was good at it. He was uncommonly successful, he liked to say, at being the sort of failure who needed armies clashing around him to forget about himself and find his equilibrium.

In the beginning, he'd gone to war out of curiosity. He had wanted to see for himself. He did not like what he saw, but he liked having seen it, and he liked telling the stories. He kept getting prizes, but he knew that his stories made no difference. The wars just kept on going, and there was always a new one, and then another. He knew his work made no difference, and his work was his life. Why write about things that nobody should ever have to know? He despised war and he could not live without it, and for this reason, when he lost perspective – or was it when he gained it? – he despised himself.

There always came a point, in his times of withdrawal, when he noticed that he'd started writing again. Writing helped. It came in small fragments at first, half-formed thoughts that gradually fitted together into a coherent mood which he could inhabit. In this way, painstakingly, he wrote himself back into existence again, and when he recovered the ability to feel happily oblivious and insignificant in the sweep of larger forces, he did not worry about annihilation and he went back to work, back to war, doing the thing he was good at. Words got him into trouble, and words got him out of trouble.

This time, the first phrase he wrote that gave him a way out was just six words: 'Self-loathing or narcissism – what's the difference?' According to the habits of his mind, that was the strongest possible argument against his feelings of failure. A day or two later, he wrote, 'Narcissists should be shot,' and it occurred to him that if he were to shoot himself that would make a very funny suicide note. It felt good to laugh.

He asked Erika, 'Should I be shot?' She said, 'Whatever makes you happy.' He thought that was funny, too, but he could see she wasn't joking. He had succeeded in making her sick of him. He began to hate himself anew. He could not withdraw further without leaving, so he left.

'You're leaving me,' she said, and he said, 'No.' Then he said, 'But I'm not doing you any good staying.' And she said, 'No.' Then she said again, 'You're leaving me.'

He waited for her to cry, but she didn't, and that made him want to stay, but he didn't.

She said, 'Good-bye, Jerry.'

He said, 'I'll write to you.'

A few wars ago, during a firefight, a photographer friend gave him the keys to a house on an island in the Hebrides. 'Just an old pile of stones on the seashore really,' the photographer said, 'but if I don't make it, it's all yours.'

When the shooting was over the photographer said, 'You saved my life. Giving you those keys made me feel free to die, so there was no point in anyone killing me. Does that make sense?'

'No,' Jerry said. 'Well – yes and no.'

In the next war, the photographer was blown up, and Jerry inherited the stone house. He had never been to see it until now. It was just one room, with a few windows, running water and a stove. The whole island was similarly austere. There was a distillery and a shop, but most of the people had fled to America more than a century ago when they ran out of food. There were just a hundred and forty-three residents left. Jerry wasn't interested in them, which was convenient, since none of them lived near his house.

The sea was right there. The sky was right there. Behind the house, the land was peat and grass that lifted toward a distant horizon. There was nothing else there, no trees, no houses, just sky, sea, grass, peat.

Jerry kept his word to Erika. He wrote to her every day. He had always written about people. Now there were no people. He didn't want to write about himself, so he decided he would only write what he saw.

'My dear,' he wrote. 'The great blue heron comes in from the south, dropping over the pier in a steadily slowing swoop, unflapping, coasting on arched wings, lowering his awkward bulk in imperceptible increments until he's skimming the glassy low-tide shallows so closely that his silhouette appears about to merge with his reflection. Suddenly his wings jerk back, and for a moment he is standing upright in the air. Then the wings drop, and he drops with them. He takes a few stiff-legged steps in the kelp beds at the water's edge. He freezes. He waits for his prey to come to him. Now he's strutting, crouching, in pursuit of some minnow. This is how the story will end – with a kill.'

He wrote again. This time, he said, 'My darling, the sky is forty shades of grey and the sea just lightly crinkled – a stillness composed of uncountable gentle movements.'

Once, at dusk, he wrote without a salutation, 'A half dozen wild goats stand silhouetted on the rocks at the tip of the island at the mouth of the bay. A half dozen gannets are in the air, knifing high above the chop and flipping sideways into their tuck and dive – the high splash of impact blowing to foam behind them.'

He no longer felt the need to address Erika directly. He no longer felt the need to account for himself. It was enough to record what was outside him. Some days, he wrote several pages, and on some days he only wrote a single sentence. One day he wrote: 'I can see for miles and miles and miles without interruption – and interruption is the enemy of mind.'

The next day he wrote, 'The entire vast view is socked in fog, a fine drizzling mist, the sky a solid blanket the bright blue-grey of skim-milk.' That was it.

A week later, he wrote: 'The drizzle-dark skies are gashed with blue, and the light showering through the gashes flames off the lighthouse-keeper's whitewashed cottage on the far hook of Lowlandman's Bay. Every afternoon, when the sun swings west and comes from behind me, splashing over my view, there are rainbows. Some are perfect sky-high arches, some are low and almost horizontal, some are pillars of candy-coloured light, and some are just slices of prismed air – scraps of rainbow hanging in the mist. Sometimes they are near and sometimes far off, sometimes solid looking, sometimes entirely transparent. Sometimes they hang like the curtains of rain falling from a single cloud on an otherwise rainless day.'

And later that day, he wrote: 'Now this is the whipping, bright, amplified light that pilots call severe clear, light that lifts the colours and distills them and makes them absurd with gleaming exaggerated perfection. In this light a pair of swans on the grey hard sand at the water's edge is doing a mating dance. An odd ritual – they stand about a yard apart, at ninety degrees to one another, and at the same moment, in response to no discernable signal, they lower their heads abruptly to barely half an inch above the ground. Their long necks dip and curve, thrust out so that their whole bodies, from tail to beak, form the shape of a tipped-over S. It's a pose of high formality – like a pinkie extended from a dainty tea-cup. Then, all at once, the necks rise and lift and reach up to full extension, pointing straight into the sky, beaks aimed high and nearly but not quite touching one another. They quiver there, then collapse, waddle one step closer together, and repeat the whole business. It is impossible to imagine what their bird brains are going through in the course of this drill. They look devoutly unexcited. And yet, my dear, there are enough swans around to indicate that it works.'

The words, 'my dear,' had come to him naturally, without thought. He had felt happy writing them, but having written them they soon made him unhappy. At night he could not sleep until he got out of bed and drew a line through them.

He had kept his word to Erika. He had written to her

86

every day. He was aware of her when he wrote. He felt that he was addressing her. But, beyond that, he never thought of her, and he never sent her what he wrote.

After a month on the island, he packed his bag to return to the wars. That night, he wrote, 'I have been as close here to feeling free of restlessness as I ever get. Now it's dark. It's entirely still and quiet. In the morning I'll be gone, and all this will always be here.'

He did not go in the morning, and when he realised he was not going he wrote, 'The wars, too, will always be here.' He felt that he was once again his own master. When he left the island a day later, he did not take the notebook with his writings. Erika found it there the next year, when she came to see the house he'd left to her. The last thing he'd written was, 'Enough.'

Evening

KATHLEEN JAMIE

Behind the grey Paps the sun sets, tinting the clouds
mauve and powder pink; the sheeny waters of Small
Isles Bay borrow the same colours. On each rock
offshore a seal lolls; one suckling a grey pup.
Silence, but for wavelets lapping the shore, and once:
the weird, shivery cry of a red-throated diver.

The Deer Larder

JOHN BURNSIDE

The first email arrived on a Thursday evening, around nine o'clock. I remember it quite clearly, because I had spent the day at the hospital, going from one department to the next, having various tests and X-rays done before ending up back in Rheumatology, being examined by my usual doctor and a very tall, rather pretty student who hadn't quite mastered the necessary air of professional detachment. The consultant was enough for them both, though. As usual. Which is not to say that she was lacking in any way – quite the contrary, in fact. No: as always, Elizabeth Marsh – my beautiful, shrewd, faintly glamorous doctor – displayed the reassuring mix of good humour, consideration and mild irony that made me thankful I had been assigned to a female specialist rather than a man. If there is one thing that I cannot abide, it's the seriousness of male professionals.

Still, St Hubert's was a teaching hospital so, with the best will in the world, it was hard not to feel like the Elephant Man as she pointed out the various interesting features of my disease: the localised but fairly extreme psoriasis, the odd little pools of inflammation on the scan, the visibly damaged areas revealed by the X-rays, while the younger woman – whose dark hair and very blue eyes reminded me, each time our eyes met, of a girlfriend I'd had twenty years before – tried to seem unperturbed.

Of course, I knew things had worsened since my last appointment, but I had tried not to think about it too much. Some of the pain was new, but I'm a fairly old hand at this by now and I've been preparing myself for this slow fall into creaky middle age since my first bout of iritis back in the early nineties. I do my bit to keep the whole process civilised: I take an interest, I make light, I use the kind of language doctors like – which is to say, accurate and undramatic, the language of a detached observer, descriptive, neutral and, most important of all, entirely innocent of any pretence to clinical knowledge. Privately, I am fascinated by the way it all works – the body, the disease, the cause and effect, the observable phenomena, the management of pain and expectations. Still, I'm always glad to get back home and be alone again – and that night was no different. Few pleasures equal the relief that comes from locking the front door behind me, turning on the desk lamp and settling down to work. The relief, and the simple happiness.

The email arrived just as I was taking my first break. My routine is pretty consistent: I do a few pages – I write commercial film scripts, mostly for training and PR companies – then I get a pot of coffee going and check my emails. That night, it was the only item in my inbox, which was odd, because there are usually masses of minor tasks and requests to deal with. At first sight, I thought it was one of those joke mails that sometimes slip through the spam filter, a specimen of those random fragments of surreal narrative that people send out by the thousand to complete strangers – presumably for some reason known to them, though I have never been able to figure out what that reason might be. My ISP is pretty good at blocking that kind of thing, but occasionally they get through – sad little narratives of trouble and desire, of achievement and loss, always starting in the middle of the story and never reaching anything as satisfying as an end. This seemed no different, in spite of the fact that it was addressed to a specific individual, someone the sender seemed to know fairly well. But then, that might have been part of the game, part of the art, as it were.

On the other hand, this email might have ended up in my inbox because of a simple error – an address badly transcribed or mistyped after a long day's work, or a few too many glasses of wine. For some reason, I didn't delete the message right away, so I can quote it in full:

Dear Monique

Well, here I am on the island, sitting in my little study with a nice glass of – guess what? – and hammering away at the Maupassant book. Finally. Got heaps done already and I've only been here four days. I've got to *La Maison Tellier* and I still can't get over how wonderful it is – how wonderful, and how terrifying when you think of what's to come and how this book foreshadows it all.

It's beautiful here. This morning started out grey and drizzly, but by mid-afternoon it had cleared and now, in this soft, slightly pastel early evening light, it's completely still, the kind of stillness where everything seems more vivid and, at the same time, more convincing. From the window, all I can see is the flat expanse of the water, still as mercury, and the white hull of a sailing boat, moored just opposite the jetty by the one shop on the island. It's preternaturally serene, utterly calm and almost silent – yet it's changing all the time. Something is always shifting. The light, the colours, the reflections. In the evenings, the water can be periwinkle blue for half an hour or so before it darkens, smooth, though not in a hard way, like glass, but with a strange surface tension, a strange perturbability to it. Like quicksilver – yes, like quicksilver, always about to change, always on the point of shifting and, at the same time, so very smooth, so very still.

You would love it here. And I meant what I said in my last email – you really are welcome any time. It's easy enough to get here – just let me know and I'll pick you up at the ferry. I promise I won't make a big thing of it, and I'm not asking you to change your mind. Honestly. I just think it's silly for us not to be friends, don't you think?

Love
Martin

That was all. It wasn't particularly interesting, it was even slightly embarrassing, to have been given such an unexpected glimpse of Martin's sad love life. Obviously, Monique had recently dumped him, probably for someone a little less wet and, despite those assurances to the contrary, his rhapsodies about the island were intended to get her back, on any terms, if only for a few intense and awkward days. Then, of course, the arguments would begin again – I knew that scenario well enough, after all – and there would be tears, *his* probably, before the week was out. No: there was nothing very interesting about this little love story and, to be honest, the only thing that caught my attention was the mention of Maupassant. It wasn't six months since I had written a script, for an educational production company, about Maupassant and Poe, and I'd been captivated by the beauty of the man's work – a beauty that seemed to me unbearably poignant, considering how painful and squalid the life had been. Of course, if I'd been more attentive that first night, I would have seen the reference to Maupassant – the mad syphilitic who wrote one or two of the most horrifying

stories in the entire European tradition – as an obvious
clue, a pointer to the game that was about to be played.
And for as long as I could manage it, I convinced myself
that what happened next really was a game, a diversion,
like so many other diversions that one finds out there
in the cold reaches of cyberspace, where nothing is as it
seems and everything, from the latest atrocities in Gaza
or Chad to the antics of Big Brother, has the quality and
status of a diversion.

But I wasn't paying attention – on the contrary. I
was thinking about the side-effects of the new drugs I
had just been prescribed, about my diminishing skills as
a touch typist – my fingers had already started to warp
into strange shapes over the keyboard – and, most of all,
I was thinking about happiness, and about how much
time remained before the solitude I had worked so hard
to attain was transformed from a joy into a burden by the
vagaries of my far from rare disease.

For the next several days, I had no commitments – which
meant I could stay in the flat and work as and when I
liked, breaking off for coffee and a tuna sandwich, or an
old movie on DVD, before returning to my desk for one
of those small revelations that makes everything magical.
When I say *small* revelations, I'm not being overly
modest: I don't entertain big ideas, not these days anyway,
and I have no illusions about my supposed talents. I just
take what somebody else gives me – a defined project,
with clear limits and constraints – and I try to light it up,
somehow, like a medieval copyist illuminating his given
text. Maybe I wanted something else when I first started
out, but nowadays, this is enough. I work according to my

own schedule and, occasionally, I create something that shines – shines, yes, even if it's only for a few moments in a mostly workaday piece. This is as much as I am allowed by the job I have chosen to do, but it turns out to be more than enough and, even now, when my body has started to betray me in all manner of subtle, yet utterly persuasive ways, I can still be surprised by the happiness I feel when I lock myself away and get to work, knowing that I won't be interrupted. Sometimes I want to kick myself for not having arrived at this place sooner – because it took me a ridiculously long time to realise that happiness was a much simpler proposition than I had first imagined. Growing up, we think it's going to be some big event: love at first sight, say, or a brilliant career; glittering prizes; a perfect wife; beautiful, gifted children. I have none of these things, but I am comfortable and I do work that, more often than not, I enjoy, work that leaves room in my day-to-day existence for the unglamorous, apparently negligible events that, cumulatively, add up to a more or less happy life. That's why there are no novels, or plays, or Hollywood movies about happiness. It's too ordinary, and it's too slow.

The second email, followed almost immediately by the third, came three days after the first and, together, they betrayed a change of mood. That didn't surprise me – it would have been foolish of Monique to accept Martin's invitation, or even to take it seriously – but I was a little annoyed that the mistake, if it was a mistake, had been repeated. I was also somewhat embarrassed by the tone of the messages – there was an ugly desperation to them that made me a little queasy – and I deleted them immediately. I guessed that Martin had been drunk when

he wrote them and I was fairly certain that he would wake
the next morning feeling more than a little shamefaced.
I even expected to receive an apology, sooner rather than
later – and I was surprised again when it didn't come the
very next day.

The one thing that didn't occur to me was to reply
to Martin and inform him of his mistake – and, looking
back, I don't know why I didn't do exactly that. Maybe I
was embarrassed for myself, as well as for him. Maybe it
was all too close to the bone, too much of a reminder of
my own lover's folly. I didn't need any reminder of the old
days – of the lovely and self-deceived time before I came
to understand that wonderful remark of Maurois (a man
who knew a thing or two about romantic love), a remark
that has been taped to the wall next to my computer for
years now:

LE BONHEUR EST UNE FLEUR QU'IL NE FAUT PAS CUEILLIR

I think, at the time, I even considered emailing those
words to my mysterious correspondent, with a simple
explanation of what had happened – but I didn't. If I had,
I could have put this matter by and forgotten it – a choice
that, for the basest of reasons, was no longer possible after
the fourth email arrived, two days later, on a clear green
evening when the city was winding up the business of
the day and switching its lights on, one by one, silver and
cherry-red and gold, for the night to come.

It began abruptly: no greeting, no reference to the earlier
emails, no attempt at a preamble. It assumed something it
had no business to assume – or so it seemed until it occurred

to me again that this was a piece of artifice, a device to draw me into the story. Or not me, exactly – I was quite certain that I had not been targeted, as such – but the reader. Because, surely this was a fiction. Surely this was a literary game, a diversion that someone out there had devised for his own reasons – Martin, not Martin, it hardly mattered. Anybody can be anybody in cyberspace, after all – a fact that, on reflection, seems to me quite appalling now. It's all flim-flam; it's all a con. I've always disliked the telephone because I can't see the other person's face – yet for years I was happy to conduct my business almost entirely by email, where I couldn't even hear a voice, or know if it was a man or a woman, a friend or a foe, even a person or a program that I was dealing with.

I'm not sure how to tell this, the email began. You're going to think I'm crazy, or maybe you'll just put it down to too little sleep and my usual over-active imagination – and it's true, I haven't been sleeping, I've hardly slept at all since I got here in fact, but what I am about to tell you isn't some hallucination and it certainly didn't spring from my over-tired or over-active mind. In fact, it didn't come from anywhere. It was just – there. It's been there all along; I just didn't see it till now.

If you remember, I said I was going to go for a long walk to clear my head – *I didn't remember this, of course, because he hadn't said anything of the kind* – and that's where I was today, all day, walking on the old trail that runs clear across the island, up through the hills and over to the west side. The trail was made by some old one-legged patriarch from the late nineteenth century – he'd ride back and forth with his retinue all around him, surveying his domain, or stalking the deer, or whatever it was they did back then, and his people would keep it all in order, all eight or so miles of it, from the eastern shore to a high pass through the hills and then down, past waterfalls and huge, tumbled rocks to this beautiful, lonely beach on the western side. On that side, there are no roads, so the only way to get to that beach is on foot, via this old track, which is mostly just a trail through the peat now, though there are still places where you find stone walkways and sometimes there will be an old culvert, with water running under your feet, or you'll find a couple of stepping stones in a shallow burn, buried in water that can be tobacco-dark with the peat or cool and clear as the cream of the well. Only sometimes, though. The rest of the time – when the burn is deep, say, or where the old track has crumbled away, it's all about wading through waist high water, or slopping across wet peat and rushes or, worst of all, fighting your way through chest high bracken, not knowing what's in there with you, waiting to strike at your ankles or leaping unnoticed into your clothes and hair. Midges, ticks, something the local folk call keds – and who knows what else. Let's just say it's no idyll. Still, for a while I was glad I'd made the effort. It was good to be out in the air, good to be out in the open, away from the house, with its frightful, yet strangely appealing shadows.

Anyhow, I got across fine and I stood a long time on the beach, communing with whatever was out there – I'm not going to say Nature, because it wasn't that, or not in the usual sense. Of course, I thought of you, and I wished you were with me. I stood a while and looked out across the water and thought my thoughts. Then, just as I started to think about heading back, it started to rain. Nothing much, at first, just a slow, sweet smirr, more mist than rain really. Scotch mist, or something like it. It wasn't that bad and, to be honest, the ground was so wet underfoot, the paths streaming with cold water and the peat so thick and spongy, it was barely a step up from bog, so a little bit more wet wasn't going to make that much of a difference.

Well, that's what I thought to begin with. By the time I got back up on to the hill, though, it was pouring down, thick, heavy rain bouncing off my face and hands – I'd not thought to bring gloves, and my hands were suddenly freezing – so I could hardly see where I was going. The only thing for it was to put my head down and plod on, following the path where it led and trusting that I wouldn't go astray – and, of course, that was exactly what I did. I had a map, but it was useless out there and, anyway, by the time I realised how far off-track I'd gone, it was sodden through. So I just kept going, trying to remember landmarks I had seen on my way over and keeping the big hill to my right. The fairy hill, they call it, but I don't think they're thinking about the fairies in children's books. I wasn't too worried, not to begin with at least. Mostly I was just annoyed with myself for not being better prepared. But I was okay, in spite of everything. I was trying to see it as an adventure, and I was thinking about getting back to the house and getting into a nice hot bath with a big tumbler of whisky and some music on the radio.

When I first caught sight of the girl, I didn't believe she was real. I thought it was a mirage, or maybe some kind of Brocken spectre, one of those tricks of the light or the gloaming that hill walkers tell you about. I mean, what else could I think? One moment, I was alone and then, suddenly, she was there, walking beside me, step for step, through the wet peat. She had her head down – she didn't look at me, not once – but she knew I was there. She knew I was there from the first – and that was *why* her head was down, because I was there. She didn't want to look at me, she was desperately trying to pretend I wasn't there – and it came to me, why I cannot begin to think, but it came to me that she was frightened. *I* frightened her. And, God knows, she frightened me too – but what frightened me most, at that moment, was her fear. Because, at that moment, as we walked in step through the driving rain, I felt like a monster, or an apparition. That's how I still feel, now that I'm back, and neither the bath nor the whisky – not one, but four, maybe five big glasses of the stuff – can change that fact.

I don't know how long she was there, beside me. It felt like ages, but it probably wasn't and then, just as suddenly as she had come, she was gone, and I was alone again, trudging home in the rain, though at that very moment when I noticed she wasn't with me any more, I saw something – a configuration of rocks, a dark, kidney-shaped lochan in the middle-distance – that told me I wasn't far from the car park where I had started out that morning, and I pressed on, trying to tell myself that it had all been a trick of the weather, an hallucination and nothing more, born out of fatigue and confusion. An hour later, I was behind the wheel of the car: sodden, frozen, caked in mud and peat, but safe.

But here's the thing. I'm back, and I'm warm and I'm all alone behind a locked door – but I'm not safe at all, and I'm not alone, even if there's nobody here with me. And I know it sounds crazy, but I can't help thinking that something I should have left behind out there on the moor has come indoors and is hidden in the house somewhere, waiting to materialise. I'm not talking about a ghost, or some fairy creature from the old stories – I'm not even talking about that girl, I'm just – I don't know –

I know this sounds crazy, but please believe me when I say it's real. I'm not imagining it, it's here – it's here right now, somewhere at the edge of my vision, just outside the door or in a far corner of the house, and it's not something I can give a name to, but it's there and it has something to do with that girl. It's not like some ghost in a film, and it's not threatening or sinister, or not exactly. If anything, it's something more abstract than that, some disembodied current of fear or apprehension or

And that was where the message ended. In mid-sentence, just like that. Maybe he had hit the send button by accident, maybe he'd just given up trying to express what he couldn't put into words and, maybe, just maybe, something terrible had happened. Something that might bring Monique to his aid, and so begin the inevitable process of reconciliation. And then again, maybe – and as soon as the thought occurred to me, I was immediately certain that I had guessed the truth – maybe this was all part of the game: a cliffhanger in a to-be-continued serial novel, designed to keep me – Martin/Not-Martin's anonymous reader – in suspense till the next instalment arrived.

I thought again of the Maupassant reference in the first message, and I had to smile. It was, quite clearly, a literary *divertissement*, a modern-day Horla story for the virtual world – and where better to accommodate Maupassant's terrifying sliver of nothingness than in cyberspace – and no doubt it would run and run. And I have to admit, this thought came as something of a relief. I had started to dislike poor lovesick Martin in his island hideaway. He certainly struck me as someone who had no business writing a biography of Maupassant. In fact, the very idea offended me. Now that I knew he was only a character, a literary invention, I could relax. That's how it is when you have attained the fragile, or perhaps I should say provisional condition of happiness – there are so many minor events, so many possible defects to the texture of existence that place it in jeopardy. Considered in that light, it's not so hard to see why, having broken his finger, Diogenes committed suicide: a moment's happiness is enough, if it is held uncontaminated in the tide of events, but it has to be perfect. It has to be untouchable.

I fully expected another email the next morning and I was surprised when nothing out of the ordinary showed up in my inbox. But then, I told myself, perhaps that was part of the game too. Perhaps my correspondent was savouring the fact that, as a storyteller, he had all the time in the world.

Whatever the reason, the next email didn't appear until four days had passed and, when it did, it was darker, and more conventional in approach. It even reminded me of those nineteenth-century stories I had read so closely when I'd worked on the Maupassant piece, beautiful, subtle stories where the first glimmers of existentialism began to shine though the fabric of the everyday – and I recalled the pleasure I had taken in that double nostalgia, first for the monochrome, coffee and tobacco-scented nothingness-haunts-being mood of the 1950s, and then, going back in time, for the damp, slightly musty folds of bourgeois dread that prefigured it.

The email was four pages long: oddly formal, suffused with a sense of inevitable doom, it was more than a little overdone, but it had its moments, nevertheless. The best passage came when Martin – I saw him, now, as something of a dandy, a displaced *fin de siècle* poet sitting at a computer screen in an office somewhere, making up stories for an unknown reader in the off hours – described his second encounter with the girl he'd met on the moor:

You remember I told you about the odd little hut behind the house – *I didn't remember, of course, but that was of no consequence* – and how I couldn't figure out what it was. It turns out that it's a deer larder, which is to say, a place where they used to hang the carcasses of the deer when they brought them in off the moor. It's louvered all the way round, so the wind blows through the slats and dries the meat – I looked this up in a book, and it really is fascinating, how it works, how the wind blows through and the meat dries slowly, they say it's much better than a cold store, but nobody's allowed to use them anymore, because of health and safety regulations –

Anyway, the next morning after my walk on the moor, I had this sudden, almost frantic urge to see inside – only it was locked and it took me a long time to find the key. I had to search and search and then finally I found it in a drawer in the kitchen, under a pile of old rags. I don't know why it was so important to me, but it was – I had to see what it was like, I just had to.

So, I finally unlocked the door and I stepped inside. Nobody had been in there for years, everything was covered in dust and cobwebs, and there wasn't much to see, just a few hooks hanging from a beam and a heap of old sacking. It had a dirt floor, and it smelled of earth and damp and, behind it all, a subtle trace of something in a far corner, something almost sweet, like iron, or rust. There was no light, of course, and even though it was only about ten or twelve feet deep, I couldn't see into the far corner – or rather, I couldn't see clearly, though I could make out a shape, some solid object, maybe a table, set against the back wall and, on it, something that I couldn't see at all, probably just more sacking, or some other junk. There was no reason to investigate further – it was just an old shed, really – but I couldn't let it go, just like that. Something was there, and I had to know what it was.

I moved forward, slowly, careful of the dark, not at all sure what I expected to find, but I knew I would find something. About halfway across, as I came within reach of the table – and that was what it was, a long, narrow table, about three feet off the ground – I saw that what I had taken for a heap of rags was actually a body, not a deer, but a person, and then, slowly, with a sudden sense of total horror, as if I had caught myself in the commission of some vicious and perverse crime, I saw that it was the girl, the one I had seen on the moor, and I realised that she was watching me – that she had, in fact, been watching me since I'd first entered the room. And, though she didn't say anything, though she didn't cry out or even move from where she was lying, I could see that she was terrified. I wanted to say something, I wanted to reassure her, but I knew it was hopeless. Anything I said would be a lie – I don't know how I knew this but I did, I knew it as surely as I have ever known anything – whatever I said would be a lie and I knew, immediately, that she was right to be afraid. Because I really was the monster she thought I was. I really was her worst nightmare, in the flesh –

The email broke off then, and the story wasn't taken up for several days. Of course, I thought this wasn't altogether fair and it annoyed me to think that, having got me hooked, my correspondent was growing tired of his story. Then again, perhaps he had just run out ideas. Certainly I detected, in the final email, the wish for an ending, a sense that the time had come to move on – and I suppose I regretted the loss of this regular diversion. When it did come, that last message was short, and more than a little unsatisfactory. It had a cursory, almost telegrammatic quality – an air, not so much of haste, as of exhausted resignation:

Still here. I don't know why you don't answer. I never wanted –

Well, it's too late now. It's here. She is here, with me, I think forever. Can you imagine that? Forever? I couldn't have done, before, but now I can. In fact, now I can't imagine anything else.

lol

Martin

And that was where it ended. I waited a few days, to see if there would be more, then I forgot about it. I got a big, rather interesting project to work on, and I went on a special diet. The new drugs were more effective than I had expected and, all in all, life carried on as usual. I didn't think about Martin again but, once, or maybe twice at most, I dreamed about the deer larder and that terrified girl, lying silent in the darkness, and when I woke, I had to congratulate my former correspondent on having got to me, if only for a moment.

That, it would appear, was the end of Martin's story, but mine remained open – no longer told, yet still unfinished – until a certain Thursday evening, exactly three months later. I know this to be the case because I had just returned from my appointment at the hospital and, in those days, my appointments were on a three-monthly schedule. I didn't get back from town till quite late and I was feeling a little low – winter was drawing in and my hands were worse than usual – but I set to work as usual, as soon as I'd had a bit to eat and got warmed up. I had a new project to work on, something a little out of the ordinary. Something into which I was pretty sure I could work the odd small miracle and I was determined to make the most of it.

I stumbled across the story while I was on the trail of something else. That's how it happens, more often than not: the stuff that stops you dead in your tracks, the little snippets of information or narrative that seem suddenly important – those vivid, beautiful or frightening discoveries that seem life-changing – come when you're surfing the web, looking for something far more pedestrian, or even banal. As it happens, the trail I had been following had, for some time, almost no relation to my research topic and, when I came upon that final, decisive story, I read it, at first, with only passing interest. Passing interest, idle curiosity even – and then, after a line or two, a growing sense of horror. It wasn't a long article, just a quirky news item, one of those stranger than fiction pieces that you only ever half believe but can't put out of your mind for days afterwards. Usually, such pieces have an obvious whiff of exaggeration or invention about them – it's not that they are out and out lies, it's just that they are so loosely based on the known facts that they might as well be fictions. Not this one, though. This one was true, more or less. I knew that even before I knew what I was reading.

As I say, it wasn't a long piece, and it was quite badly put together, wordy and rambling and stylistically weak. Real cub reporter stuff. In short, it told the story of a man who had been found, naked and alone and quite obviously mad, squatting on a raised beach on the isle of Jura. Someone had seen him from a ferry boat and called the police; subsequently, the man, who could not or would not speak and appeared not to have eaten or slept for some time, was taken to a hospital on the mainland, where he was later identified as Martin Crisp, a university lecturer from Reading, who had been renting a house on the island over the summer. The piece concluded with two quotes: the first, from a local man, who said that Mr Crisp had been touched by the fairies, and it would be a long time before he ever came right, the second, from one of the hospital staff, who said that Mr Crisp was still unable to speak but, though it was obvious that something terrible had happened to this man, there was no clinical reason for his condition. When asked to elaborate further, the doctor – whose name, by what seemed to me a chilling coincidence, was Elizabeth Marsh – remarked that she had never before had a case quite like this one. 'It's not that Mr Crisp *can't* talk,' she said – and I pictured my own Dr Marsh saying this – 'but it seems to me that he's said what he wanted to say and now he's waiting for his answer.'

Corran sands

KATHLEEN JAMIE

Between the emergency airfield and the sands
tangle extravagent numbers of wildflowers: foxgloves
wander on maddened journeys toward death,
gorse pods pop in the afternoon heat. Purple grasses,
yellow rattle, eyebright, hawksweed, ragwort, clover,
devil's bit scabious, spires of purple loostrife,
bird's foot trefoil, knapweed, frothy meadowsweet,
(must be a damp bit) orchids, speedwell, dandelion
- and feeding on nettles, a squad of black caterpillars,
speckled silver, like a starry night in winter.

Tissue Sample

WILL SELF

'Tissue Sample', or maybe 'The Tissue of Culture', were both titles I considered in the first few days after arriving on the island of Jura, for a story I intended to write some time in the future – after the book I was currently working on was done. I toyed with 'The Biopsy' as well. I made notes for this story when I went for walks along the island's sole road, then continued as I speared into the interior over sodden tussocks and between granite outcrops. More notes were made, sitting at a vantage where I could see the peaks encircling a hammered pewter loch. I made these notes, and then picked up bits of quartz while squinting back to the mainland across the sound. It all felt a little hopelessly profound. I was high on the beauty of the open spaces; and, as ever, in these land-scapes of the far north the clouds – white, pink, purplish – inverted the big picture by cushioning the hilltops, so that the land seemed to repose on top of them.

I'm used to solitude – I have no problem with it. Young people say they want to write, and I ask them: 'Are you prepared for decades of solitary confinement?' I'm accustomed to the prison farming of prose production, the scattering of mixed seed – ideas, aperçus, images, descriptions, tropes, fragments of dialogue – on the harrowed field of the unconscious; then its careful husbandry through rituals of manual labour: first draft first thing in the morning; breakfast; second draft until lunch; walk; supper; retyping into the evening.

I count cigarettes, cups of tea and biscuits; I sleep with a notebook by my pillow; my chance ruminations and ejaculations are instantly caught. My meals are taken at the worktable; cutlery clinking loud, while my mastication is thorough and old mannish. As a child I wondered why I found the scenes in *2001* in which the ancient astronaut eats dinner on Ganymede, in his dressing gown, viewed by his younger self, to be the most haunting – now I know, it was a precognition of this state, at once oneiric and profoundly real, wherein, shorn of the quotidian, narratives take on a teasing verisimilitude.

In the past I had to have this time alone, either at the outset of a book, or towards its completion. I liked to go somewhere remote and preferably close to the sea; I kidded myself that the tide, instead of salting the fields of the unconscious, tugged at the germinating shoots of stories, pulling them into the light of day. Islands were good, because they are discrete and legible – in the way that books are.

I've never known, especially, the tyranny of the blank page, but the background hum of the ephemeral – tinny news broadcasts crumpled up in the ear; printed fish-and-chip paper; the bleep, trill and locust-nibble of phones, faxes and computers – these assailed me. And then there were those more substantial hauntings, the revenants of responsibility – my partners, our children – and the cheesy ghost-busters I zapped them with – drugs and alcohol.

Nowadays I find I can work in the bosom of my family, in the heart of London – so this sojourn, three weeks on the Hebridean island of Jura – was a bonus.

True, I would be late delivering the novel I was writing if I didn't knuckle down, but I didn't *have* to be there. That first night in the Jura distillery lodge, wandering the vast apartments with their absurd decorative scheme – antlers on the walls, antlers for shelf brackets, antler chairs and candlesticks – I recalled other, less voluntary exiles. More than a decade before, holed up at my late friend Christopher Bowerbank's house, Viera Lodge on the Orcadian island of Rousay, unable to sleep, glugging down his cherry slivovitz, because I'd already done for vodka, the gin and naturally – the whisky.

My body was anaesthetised but my mind still scampered up the ancient walls as I planned each stage of the journey – car to jetty, small ferry to Orkney mainland, car across to Stromness, big ferry out through Scapa Flow to the Scots mainland, then the deranged drive down the A9 to the first town big enough to have a heroin dealer.

It wasn't like that anymore – I'd been sober for years. When the writer's residency was offered to me it came with expenses, a decent stipend, the mad living quarters and 'as much whisky as you can drink', courtesy of the distillery, who were co-funding it. I'd never taken a writer's residency of this kind before: I didn't need anyone to help me go to creative jail, and I was fortunate enough to be able to afford my own barbed wire – psychic, or otherwise. But the prospect of Jura was tempting: there was the connection with George Orwell and the writing of *Nineteen Eighty-Four*; the beautiful Paps – conical 1950s breasts of hills – the wilderness of the west of the island, with its curious raised beaches, its wild goats, and boat-swallowing whirlpools. Besides, I'd long wanted to spend time in the Hebrides, now that Christopher was dead and

Viera Lodge in other hands, there was less to command my loyalty to Orkney, why shouldn't I find another Ganymede to have dinner on?

The Paps had an odd quality – being, under certain lights, heart-achingly ethereal, while under others as ugly as slag heaps. It was the same with the Laird, who, in late evening, under the autumnal glow of a down light gained the roseate glow he must have possessed as a youth: the jowls fell from his cheeks, the bags were hefted from beneath his eyes, his lips plumped-up redly.

I make no apology for the 'redly', these are notes, transcribed verbatim. I unpacked my bags and created a simulacrum of my work room at home: at the end of the main table I set out my Olivetti 22 and the various drafts of the work in progress, together with dictionary, thesaurus etc. The laptop went on another table, facing down on to the distillery yard. I found a standard lamp with spotlights that I could angle on to my pages, and in the music room – preposterous, with a chaise longue and a lovers' sofa – I found a music stand that would do to hold the hand-corrected drafts when I was retyping.

In the corner of the main room stood an enormous fridge built from paradoxically warm-toned hardwood. Later, Catriona, the young woman who looked after the lodge, told me it was made in Brazil, in the 1920s. It had an engine on top of it that hammered into life every so often then underscored the emptiness of the apartment with its chilly beat. I didn't mind the fridge – I've never minded them. In my first novel, *My Idea of Fun*, I had my psychopathic antihero, Ian Wharton, sitting in the late night kitchen, and musing on the possibility of releasing an album called *20 Great Fridge Noise Hits*. I've always liked those sounds that, plangent at first, insinuate themselves so thoroughly that you become quite unconscious of them until, suddenly, they cease – a bit like life.

As for his lady (find correct term for female laird), her beauty was always unimpeachable in Magnus's eyes – never sullied by frowsty bedchamber or foetid chamber pot.

The seed of 'Tissue Sample' was given to me by Marc Quinn; in February of that year the artist and I had travelled to Easter Island in the Pacific, to see the famous *moai*, the giant stone statues that were the votive objects for a civilisation that thrived for half a millennium on this, the remotest inhabited island in the world. Marc was a good companion in all sorts of ways – engaged, enthusiastic, precise – he also shares my thematic, as well as having – rare in a visual artist – a strong sense of narrative progression. In a few evenings with Marc, sitting eating ceviche on the terrace of a luxury eco-hotel, I was able to sketch out the scenarios for the six stories that would comprise my collection *Liver*. I began writing this story cycle in the autumn of that year – when I'd finished *The Butt*, the novel I was writing on Jura; however, there were two outlines I discarded, of which 'Tissue Sample' was one. Needless to say, all the stories had a bilious tinge.

The mainland hills would deliquesce in the showers blown down the sound.

Marc and I had known a man called Sam Finch when we were both racketing around Soho's drinking clubs in the early 1990s. Finch had a bad rep' that somewhat belied his schtick as mine host – he at one time managed Lawrence's, a well-known wine bar on Lexington Street, later he went on to found Gray's, the private members' club opposite the Groucho. It was said of Finch – who had stuck with the tweedy raiment of his squirearchical

Norfolk background – that he had killed a man; although as I heard it this was a grotesque embellishment, mere Chinese restaurant whispers, and the death had been a lunge out the window of the flat above the wine bar; a space walk taken by an acidnaut who wanted to get higher. Finch, the kaleidoscopes of LSD rammed in his deep-set eyes, only looked on, an accessory to suicide – but then, aren't we all?

Whatever the truth, Finch did little to dispel the sulphurous haze that hung about him, a miasma that – according to Marc – derived from his very peculiar upbringing in marshy East Anglia.

The double doors, the inset turrets, the castellated fake battlements, the equally fake moat – all of these features served to both compress and shrink the castle, making it appear hardly larger than a conventional, middle-class establishment.

On the remote Norfolk estate where Finch was born, lived his choleric farmer father and his miserably lusty mother. A tutor was engaged early on for the boy, and in time-honoured fashion Finch's mother took him as a lover. In due course she became pregnant, and this being before the legal availability of abortion, she and the tutor conceived an unusual plan to hoodwink Squire Finch. Both the tutor and the squire were amateur scientists – or rather hokey experimenters, who liked nothing better than messing around with plant hybrids, or shaving rabbits to see if they'd survive myxomatosis. When the child was born – another boy – the tutor put it to the squire that it might be interesting to experiment on his sons, by feeding one of them exclusively on meat, and the other on vegetables, in order to see if this made any difference to their eventual development.

Squire Finch took the bait and the boys suffered their unusual diets, the older – despite his Ghandi mush of pulses and leaves, growing into the spitting image of his red-faced father; the younger – no matter how many barons of beef were inserted into him – coming ineluctably to resemble the flaxen-haired and ethereal tutor . . . At least, that's how I see it – but I'm embellishing already; Marc didn't know whether Finch was the older or the younger son, but for narrative purposes I'm assuming that this is a tale he told himself, and that he was the older son – and rightful heir – who, since opposites invariably attract, had been disinherited by Squire Finch, in favour of his carnivorous favourite: the tutor's bastard.

Lady Alys was bewitching – and he was bewitched by the smooth geometry of her Slavic cheekbones, by her enamel-blue eyes, and by the tips of her curiously angled ears, that – like the antlers of the indigenous stags – were swept back, suggesting that even when at rest, she was moving at a great velocity.

I piled my books on the low coffee table – a slab of ersatz driftwood – under the hundred points of the pointless ornamental antlers. There was a full suit of armour in the corner, painted with what seemed to be white emulsion. This, the main room, consisted of the kitchen – with the aforementioned Depression-era fridge – a large seating area, and a separate embayment that could be closed off with double smoked-glass doors: the music room. Down two flights of stairs five large bedrooms were ranged along a broad corridor, each one had a different pile of tat in it – steamer trunks in one, hatboxes in the next. The end bedroom had a freestanding bath, white drapery and seashells on the coffered mantelpiece. It had a good vibe – so I took it, hoping the marine motif would work its way into my unconscious. In truth, the whole lodge had a good atmosphere. I learned later that Bambi Sloan, the perfectly named interior decorator, had imported five tonnes of stuff to stock the capacious apartment, and while the boho-baronial interiors were risible they were also – despite their carnage-as-ornamentation – oddly cheery.

I unpacked my clothes and put them away in the chest of drawers, meditating on the deer – and Jura, which it is believed, derives its name from the Norse name for same. Coming off the wee ferry that had brought me across from Islay to the jetty at Feolin, I had driven straight into herd of red deer, their limbs, antlers and long faces forming a thicket in the roadway, agitated by the zephyr of instinct. There had been other people on the ferry, and now the cars and pickups nudged their way through the deer, then spaced out along single-track road that twisted along the shoreline, then rose and fell over the spurs of the hills, towards the village of Craighouse. Mizzle and dusk.

Base the laird on Evans – he is one-legged, with nutty theories about deer husbandry and the livers of deer. His wife is bored and longs to feel two legs threshing between her own.

I've no idea whether the story about Finch – the Soho boulevardier who used to startle us West End sots by pulling a brace of pheasant from the poacher's pocket of his old tweed jacket – was apocryphal or not. It seemed more like a nineteenth-century tale to me, than a factual account of something that took place in the fifties. I could imagine the landowner as an eccentric Scottish laird, a godless disciple of T H Huxley in a Highland morass of Wee Frees, who was prone to measuring the skulls of his tenants and comparing the spidery data with the ape skulls he'd brought back from his time as a district commissioner in Africa. Callipers would figure.

Easter Island was a small triangle of believably temperate lushness; if I narrowed my eyes a little more the grassy hyper-mounds of its extinct volcanoes became credible *beinns*. Shorn of its giant palms by its clans of competitive sculpture builders, the hankie of grass, eucalyptus and fig scrub was now overrun by mangy horses. The long modern history of genocidal incursions, the diaspora and return of the rump of its inhabitants – in the 1930s it was even a sheep station, overseen no doubt by Scotsmen – all this made it a believable transliteration, in the cobalt Pacific, of Jura in the aquamarine Atlantic.

I read up on the island. The biggest and seemingly most authoritative book, *Jura: Island of Deer*, was by Peter Youngson, who had been the Church of Scotland minister there from 1975 to 1988. Predictably, once I got talking to a few of the islanders they had tales of his boundless quirkiness – but then that's remote and sparsely populated islands for you, they're all Lilliputs of conformity, populated by Brobdingnagian eccentrics.

In Youngson's book I found Henry Evans, who established his own 'deer forest' on the island in the 1860s, and who took an increasingly intense interest in the animals. Quoting from Youngson: 'In 1890 (Evans) privately printed the result of his obsession with the red deer of Jura. The booklet was simply entitled *Some Account of Jura Red Deer* and ran to thirty-eight pages. Evans recorded everything he possibly could about the red deer he was shooting – their ages, weights, numbers, breeding success, parasites, causes of death. He compared everything he could about their presence on the various parts of the island. It makes for dull reading, with its endless tables of weights and sizes.'

He also only had one leg, which necessitated his moving about the rugged terrain on a pony. He had his workers blaze a trail for him, so he could ride across the spine of the island, then down Glen Batrick to Loch Tarbert, the great seawater notch in Jura's western flank. Inevitably, I associated Evans with another Jura resident with one leg, Bill Dunn, who in the 1940s was the tenant of Kinauchdrach, the farm to the north of Orwell's Barnhill, and who wooed then married the writer's older sister, Avril. It was said of Dunn that despite his handicap he had swum across the notorious Gulf of Corryvreckan to the north of the island.

The amputee laird, obsessed by deer to the detriment of his lustful wife; the right period: the late nineteenth century – you can see the direction my thoughts were taking: here was the proper milieu for the story about Finch that Marc Quinn had related to me on Easter Island.

Victor, the tutor, had been a medical student in Edinburgh, but he couldn't cope with the dissections – the sex with the Lady Alys frees him from his sense of bodily revulsion. He feels marvellously at peace, either with his head lying between her breasts, or upon the heather between the Paps. He goes up there to walk and to paint watercolours.

There was cock-a-leekie soup and crackers in the larder, pomegranate juice in the Brazilian fridge. Under the antlers I ate supper on Ganymede, then went across to the pub to get a bar of chocolate. I was wary of talking to anyone – I'm naturally wary anyway. All those years of solitary confinement mean that my inclination, on seeing anyone I know, is to cross to the other side of the road. Besides, no longer being a drinker I lacked the obvious velcro of sociability: the loss of inhibition that makes one psyche hook into the eyes of another. So, it was grunts in the bar of the Jura Hotel. Only one man spoke to me that evening, he was hunched in the entrance to the public bar, thin-faced with greasy-grey collar-length hair. I'd noted him earlier, staring down from the front window of the distillery lodge: he'd been in and out of the pub all evening: in to drink, out to smoke another cigarette. Up close he had the face I expected: grazed, buffeted – at once preserved and rotted by alcohol. His eyes swam towards the top of it, wearing an expression at once bemused and amused. He was friendly enough, muttering some slushiness to the effect that: was I the writer who was come to the island? And after I'd conceded that I was we parted.

I don't want to make too much of this, I was, after all, a recovering alcoholic writer who'd just moved into an apartment above a whisky distillery – fair whisky, that once I'd loved: with her peaty-blonde, mind-captivating tresses   so it's not unsurprising that I sought, psychically, to distance myself from him, but even so, I'd swear to it, that night in the gloaming, the chilly cloak of death seemed to lie on the man's shoulders as he drew on his cigarette.

Victor doesn't go on Evans's walk – he can't bear to tread in the other man's groove; although they get on perfectly well, what with their shared interest in phrenology, heredity and the work of Francis Galton. Evans has, himself, undertaken a variation of Galton's experiment into the nature of religious belief. Whereas Galton worshipped a figure of Punch *every day for a month, the laird made obeisance before the head of a stag nailed to the wall of his pocket-baronial hall. Galton subsequently found himself unable to enter his Pall Mall club without feeling an uncontrollable urge to get down on his knees before the table covered with magazines and periodicals – including* Punch *– but the Laird's automatic compliance is to the bizarre experiment that the tutor proposes, once it becomes clear that Lady Alys is pregnant for the second time.*

Looking back over my notebooks for that first week on Jura is to undertake an archaeology of the creative process: there are the straightforward nature notes, remarking on the herons in Small Isles Bay, the clarity of the seawater, the wild irises and primroses nodding along the verges, the hooded crows skulking on the dry stone walls of the small fields, the slash of the wind across the still brown silk of a lochan. Workmanlike comments concerning the novel in hand are brief and to the point: 'No anaesthetic for the CUT only engwegge'; 'Some blacks get the CUT – not *all* – they are respected, MAKKATAS and such.'

Then there were the little gobbets of 'Tissue Sample', a story I already saw as performing two functions: fulfilling the condition of my residency at the distillery lodge, and forming part of *Liver*, a story cycle in which each distinct narrative was a flow of blood or bile through the largest organ of the human body. It was easy enough to push the vestigial tale in this direction.

Alys fooled the laird the way women always do. Victor was in agony when she slept with her husband, yet Alys gained strength: the laird's single leg between her thighs felt like an enormous, jointed and muscular penis.

A couple of days after I'd arrived on Jura I went across to the Stores – which were housed in a small whitewashed building between the distillery and the sea – to discover an uneasy and shocked atmosphere. The man I'd exchanged a few words with on the evening I arrived had, it transpired, dropped dead – and it was one of the young women who worked in the stores who'd found his body. He was only in his early fifties.

Victor, the tutor, can be a vehicle for my own ambivalence about the rich. He sees the island as being like a butcher's diagram of an animal carcase – divided up into shooting estates. In his heart of hearts Victor is a believer in Proudhon's dictum that property is theft – he once took tea with Kropotkin – so how can land be owned?

I say 'it transpired', but it didn't transpire for quite a while: I was still keeping my distance from the islanders, typing away up in the apartment, while down below I could hear the heavy rumbling of whisky casks in the bowels of the distillery. It was several days before I remarked upon that subdued atmosphere – and then the funeral was nearly upon us: a foregathering of black suits and skirts at the Jura Hotel – relatives from Ireland and further afield, who, on stepping outside for a cigarette, emulated the last hours of the man they'd come to mourn.

The novel was consuming most of my energies. The scattering of mixed seed had been mostly abandoned for ploughing along, line after line. Besides, I'd already realised that 'Tissue Sample' wasn't going to sit that well with the rest of the story cycle I'd devised. The equivalent, for Victor, of Finch's tutor's experiment, was to have the bastard child fed exclusively on the livers of the laird's beloved red deer. So it would be, that this child would grow up tall and straight and keen – while the rightful heir, fed on heavy, late Victorian stodge, became as gouty and rotund as his father. The link to *Liver* (the working title of the story cycle) was the deer's livers – and the alcohol; because of course the disaffected rightful heir would leave the island when his half-brother inherited, and end up a drunk on the mainland. *See you, pal, I fucking love you!* An obnoxious drunk in a Glasgow bar like a urinal, who corners a chance passer by, who's only come in to use the gents, and subjects him, while his bladder bulges, to this awful tale.

Or rather: *It's a story within a story. There's an old Scots writer, dying of cirrhosis, who tells his young amanuensis of a story that he couldn't use, that in turn was told to him by a man he met in the 1960s who was dying of cirrhosis; this was the tale of the man's father, who had also died of cirrhosis, and who had been the rightful laird of the shooting estate on Jura.* Thus displacing the tale back further in time, and deeper into the mythopoeic landscape of the Hebrides. Which is what I've done anyway, I suppose, by not writing a story as such, but rather, writing the story of a story that was never written: its genesis, evolution and demise. But then that's the greatest thing about the creative sphere; unlike that of distillation or deer stalking: nothing is ever lost in the economy of ideas.

Twenty One Year Old

LIZ LOCHHEAD

On our first night at Jura Lodge you say:
'here's a bottle of the Twenty One Year Old,
hey Lizzie, let's taste . . .' and we toast
– once we've managed to track two nip glasses down –
'oh *there* they are, Tom –
of *course*, my deah, on the de*can*-
ter tray, mayhap, in the *Music* Room!' I laugh,
oh I have to, as you slosh us each
a generous inch or more of gold, yes
you clink your glass with mine
and we toast
our good fortune and the holiday to come.

All holidays
are whole small lives lived somewhere else.
And all lives consist, in part, of habits
but we don't yet know this will be
one of the habits of this holiday –
on the long
light
nights of July
to sit astride that pair of purple velvet stools in the big
bay window of the Music Room looking out to the bay
with our
big brand new sketch books balanced before us and

something more than twenty one years
old and easy-listening
playing – like old Van Morrison
predicting *it's a marvellous night for a moondance*
or Dylan groaning out *tangled up in blue*
as I scrabble for that and every other colour, for
on the little gaming table between us
a jumble of oil pastels and coloured conté crayon
is rolling around our rested whisky glasses –
occasionally savoured and sipped from,
but never refilled –
as busily, fluently, more or less silently,
we sketch and scratch away and scribble
not stopping till – late – all the last of the light is gone
and we can't see
either what we're drawing or the marks we've made.

It'll be tomorrow
before I can enjoy the garish gladhanded sweep
you've made of a bit of the bay and pier and shrug
to see how hopeless was my
daft task of putting down the ever-changing sky
with its bands and streaks and shifting clouds
and almost every colour
except
sky blue.
But in spite of what
– on paper – neither of us captured
neither of us I'd bet
has ever been happier or easier with a crayon in our hands
since we were five years old –
nor less self-critical about the outcome, so

we can look at the nothing much we've caught
('happiness writes white' said Philip Larkin) and
remember how lovely was last night's peace
watching the always eventful nothing happening
as the light spilled from the pool room of the hotel
and the players' movements went like fiddlers elbows,
how now and then one person,
sometimes joined by another, then another
might linger by the back door with a smoke
and how – till it got too dark –
you could
see the laughter you were far too far away to hear.

The Whiskies

Whisky Distilling
on the Island of Deer

CHARLES MACLEAN

It would be safe to suppose that whisky distilling has taken place on Jura since time immemorial, although there is no written evidence.

I say this because Jura's was a pastoral economy – Highland cattle were the staple items of trade and wealth until the mid nineteenth century, when sheep came to dominate. As happened elsewhere in the Highlands, 'the beasts' were brought indoors during the hard winter months and kept alive with the residues of brewing and distilling, the husks and spent grains, known as 'draff'. The secrets of distilling had been known on neighbouring Islay since at least the 1490s, and possibly for two centuries before that.

Jura itself is the wildest island in the Inner Hebrides: a huge area of rock and blanket bog, most of it without roads or habitation of any kind. It was not easy to grow crops on such terrain; some oats were grown, and a dwarf barley called bere, but most were imported from Islay and Kintyre. From early times sparse human habitation clung to the east coast, evidenced today by mysterious megaliths and standing stones. On the west side, a small clachan once existed at Ruantallan, at the mouth of Loch Tarbert, and another at Glengarrisdale in the north-west corner of the island until it was abandoned in 1947. Here there is a cave which, until about thirty years ago, contained some bones and a skull belonging to a Maclean who was killed when the perfidious Campbells attacked the island in 1647, during the Wars of the Covenant.

As more than one writer has observed: 'On Jura it is easy to believe that there is no such thing as the human race.' Such humans who did live there will have been glad of a drop of whisky!

Distilling for private consumption (i.e. not for sale) was perfectly legal until 1781. After this it was summarily banned – which simply meant that people did it covertly. Jura is famous for its many caves, and it seems likely that such places were used by the 'smugglers'. Certainly, there is a strong tradition that a cave at Craighouse, close to the site of the present Isle of Jura Distillery, was used for such purpose. In 1810 a rudimentary distillery was erected outside the cave, by the owner of the island, Archibald Campbell. In its early days, this small distillery may have been operated by David Simson, the founder of Bowmore Distillery on Islay, and the true 'father' of legal distilling on that island.

Campbell's new buildings included a maltings, to convert barley into malt. The 'green malt' itself was dried over locally cut peats, which will have imparted a smoky taste, not unlike that found in such Islay malts as Lagavulin, Ardbeg and Laphroaig. The first licensee we know of is William Abercrombie in 1831, but he only had it a year, handing over to Archibald Fletcher.

'The Small Isles Distillery', as it was named, would remain in Fletcher hands for twenty years, but they didn't make much of a success of it. They were owing rent by 1835, and by the time they gave up had only 5,450 litres of whisky in bond – and this of doubtful reputation.

Campbell's factor tasted some of Fletcher's 'best aged whisky' in 1851, and showed it to the manager of Caol Ila Distillery, '. . . who makes the best whisky on Islay. I could not get him to express himself as to whether Jura could be improved or not, he merely said old or new it retained its former taste ...'

The laird thought of selling the distilling equipment for scrap: the copper and brass were valued at £400, and the whole plant at £600. The day was saved, however, when he was approached by a Mr Buchanan from Glasgow, who signed a lease on condition that he be supplied all the peat he needed from the estate, and that local farmers would take up all the draff. In spite of also taking the lease of Caol Ila Distillery, Buchanan went bust within ten years. His successors in the Small Isles Distillery lasted a mere four years.

In 1876 a thirty-four-year lease was signed between the then laird, James Campbell, and James Fergusson & Sons of Glasgow. The Fergussons invested some £25,000 in improvements to the distillery, increasing capacity to 817,000 litres of spirit per annum, and making it 'one of the easiest worked distilleries in the district', according to the indomitable traveller, Alfred Barnard, who visited in 1886. The Fergussons also undertook to build a pier capable of taking vessels of ten-foot draught at low water, and constructing a road, a bridge and a waiting room on the pier head.

But relations between them and the laird were not good. There had been some angry exchanges in the mid 1890s, and when James Campbell died in 1901, to be succeeded by his son, the Fergussons quit Jura, taking with them all their new plant and machinery, and gradually removing their stocks of mature whisky. They continued to pay rent until the expiry of the lease in 1918, but Colin Campbell pursued them for repairing the pier – estimated at £1,293, while the Fergussons felt that £67 was closer to the mark! – plus a further £1,000 for dredging the harbour. It is not known whether this dispute was ever settled, but it marked the end of distilling on Jura for many years.

Before World War I the population of Jura was over a thousand; by the 1950s it was down to 150 souls. World War II had taken its toll, and as with many Hebridean islands, there had been a steady drift of younger people away to the mainland. Ownership was now in the hands of Robin Fletcher (of Ardlussa Estate in the north – no relation to the distilling Fletchers, so far as I am aware), Tony Riley-Smith (of Jura Estate in the south) and three others. As the focal point of a wide-ranging plan to increase employment on the island and attract new blood, Fletcher and Riley-Smith determined to rebuild the distillery.

This made sound commercial sense. Demand for Scotch whisky had never been greater. Up and down the land distilleries were being refurbished and expanded, and new ones built. Backing for the project came from Scottish & Newcastle Breweries and the old established blending house, Charles Mackinlay & Company. In 1956 the landowners secured the services of William Delmé-Evans, who had built Tullibardine Distillery at Blackford, near Gleneagles, from scratch between 1947 and 1949.

In an interview in 2004, shortly before his death, Delmé-Evans recalled: 'During 1958 I started designing a new distillery which just about trebled the production capacity of the old one, and by 1963 Jura Distillery was commissioned.' He used the same sloping site as the previous distillery, clearing the crumbling remains of the former, except for the manager's house – the tall building on the right, when viewed from the sea. The water came from the same source as previously – the Market Loch.

'My primary aim was to construct an economic distillery within the space available,' he wrote. 'Everything had to be simple and fall to hand. You could not afford to complicate things in so remote a location . . . It was our intention to produce a Highland-type malt differing from the peaty stuff last produced in 1900. I therefore designed stills to give spirit of a Highland character, and we ordered malt which was only lightly peated.'

The first single malt from the new distillery was released in 1974, but the huge majority of the make went for blending (much of it to Mackinlays). One of the reasons for wanting to produce a 'Highland-style' of whisky was that this was more desired by the blenders than the smoky 'Islay-style'. Of course, the latter is now very popular with whisky drinkers around the world, and in response to this demand, Jura has, since 2002, offered a smoky style called 'Superstition'.

In 1976 Delmé-Evans was succeeded as managing director by Dr Alan Rutherford of the distillery company, with Don Raitt as manager. They immediately set about replacing the worn-out plant and making improvements in efficiency, as well as expanding the stillhouse from two to four stills. Capacity was increased to 2.5 million litres of spirit per annum. Dr Rutherford went on to become Head of Production at United Distillers, emeritus Professor of Distilling at Heriot Watt University and a Lieutenant Colonel in the Parachute Regiment (T.A.).

Ownership of Jura Distillery passed to Invergordon Distillers in 1985, then Whyte & Mackay ten years later, when that company was owned by American Brands (later called Jim Beam Brands). In 2001 Whyte & Mackay was bought out by its management for £200 million. John Bulman was manager from 1984 until 1990, succeeded by Willie Tait, 1990 to 2002, and by Michael Heads, 2002 to the present.

Since 1995 Richard Paterson, Master Blender at Whyte & Mackay, and a legend in the whisky trade, has been responsible for production at the distillery, and for deciding which whiskies to bottle as Isle of Jura single malt.

The making of malt whisky is a kind of alchemy, and the way each distillery transmutes the base material (malted barley) into liquid gold is unique to itself, and relies upon tradition and high craft. Delmé-Evans set the style; the men I mention above continue the work, and the skills they employ are little changed from those of the illicit distillers on the Isle of Jura. What a comfort is malt whisky!

Main References
Neil Wilson, *The Island Whisky Trail* (Neil Wilson Publishing, 2003)
Gavin Smith, *The Whisky Men* (Birlinn, 2005)
Charles MacLean, *Scotch Whisky: A Liquid History* (Cassell, 2003)
Hamish Haswell-Smith, *The Scottish Islands* (Canongate, 1996)
Alfred Barnard, *The Whisky Distilleries of the United Kingdom* (Harper's, 1887)

CURRENT BOTTLINGS OF ISLE OF JURA
SINGLE MALT SCOTCH WHISKY

The core range is bottled at 10, 16 and 21 years old (all at 40% volume), with Superstition (a mix of 13- and 20-year-old malts, at 45% volume), and 'Legacy' (a mix of 10-year-old and older whiskies, at 40%, sold only in duty-free outlets). Richard has also selected special casks and parcels of casks for limited edition bottling, including the '1984 – George Orwell Edition' (a 19-year-old at 42% volume, from two different kinds of sherrywood – 800 cases only), 30-year-old bottlings from 1973, 1974 and 1975 (all single casks at cask strength in very limited amounts) and a 36-year-old from 1965 (which yielded 449 bottles at 44% volume).

The character of Jura's new make spirit reminds one of pine-sap and gorse flowers, with traces of cinnamon and a hints of ozone – like sea-breeze. Remember, the malt is unpeated, so the whisky is closer to the Highland style than that of Islay, where the 'typical' character is pungent, smoky, peaty and medicinal. Jura is an easy, friendly, unchallenging whisky; a classic 'island' malt (with maritime notes and salty sea-spray).

The casks in which the whisky is matured make a huge contribution to mellowing and filling out the original character of the new make.

Here are my thoughts on the core range of ages:

Isle of Jura 10 Years Old
The wood here is 100% American white oak; this has developed the piney notes in the whisky, and the coconut/gorse flower aromas. It has added various other floral

elements, yet it has not dominated the original character, and the light spicy/cinnamon notes remain. An easy drinking, all day malt.

Isle of Jura 16 Years Old
Ninety per cent of the casks used for this expression are of European oak, and have previously contained sherry. These casks have introduced a hazelnut/crushed almonds/soft marzipan note to the aroma, together with some orange peel, but still with sea-spray in the background. Warm and friendly; ideal for early evening enjoyment.

Isle of Jura 21 Years Old
This is a mix of 100% European oak, ex-Oloroso sherry casks, and the flavour is given greater depth, colour and complexity both by the wood and the extra age. There is a curious mint-tea aroma to start with, and then the familiar marzipan and orange peel – but now richer and softer. Huge complexity. Add only a very little water and hold the spirit in the mouth before swallowing: Richard Paterson always recommends that you hold it for a second a year – so in this case 21 seconds – before you swallow! An after dinner dram.

With thanks to Richard Paterson, Master Blender, and Michael Heads, Manager, Isle of Jura Distillery.

CHARLES MACLEAN began writing about Scotch whisky twenty-five years ago, and has published nine books on this subject to date including *Malt Whisky* (Mitchell Beazley, 1997) which has been translated into ten languages, and *Whisky: A Liquid History* (Cassell, 2003), which won Wine & Spirits Book of the Year (2005) in the James Beard Awards, the most prestigious American gastronomic prize. He was the founding editor of *Whisky Magazine* and is 'British Editor' of the Russian glossy *Whisky*. He has been Contributing Editor of the Scotch Malt Whisky Society's *Newsletter* (where he also chairs the Nosing Panel and writes the tasting notes) since 1995. He is also whisky correspondent for *Scottish Field*, *Scottish Life* (U.S.A.) and *SCOTS* (Australia).

He was trained in 'the sensory evaluation of potable spirits' by the Scotch Whisky Research Institute in 1992 and has presented numerous tastings and talks in the U.K. and abroad. He is a member of the Judging Panel (Spirits) of the International Wines & Spirits Competition, and Whisky Consultant to Bonhams Auctioneers. He was elected a Keeper of the Quaich, the industry's highest accolade, in 1992 for 'his services to Scotch whisky over many years'.

Spirit of the Island

RICHARD PATERSON, MASTER BLENDER

I am often asked which my favourite single malts are. I have fallen in love with many. But one consistently stimulates and excites me, and is truly as individual as they come. That malt is Isle of Jura. Although I have never lived on Jura, I have, over the years, visited it on many occasions. It encompasses all of the things I love most. Stunning Scottish scenery, exciting walks, birds of prey, history, wonderful people and, of course, a fabulous distillery.

One hundred and nineteen distilling sites have been identified on Jura, an extraordinarily large number for a comparatively small island. Distilling is said to have been carried on in caves close to Craighouse, and may have been taking place as far back as the 1600s. Accurate information is hard to come by, but the site of the present distillery, owned by the Campbell lairds, was probably first used for whisky-making around 1810.

Over the years the distillery has had varying fortunes – until the modern era when, in August 1991, it became part of the Whyte & Mackay group. From a personal point of view, I was excited to have a single malt of such individuality at my disposal, but I was also looking to the longer term, where I could see older expressions of Jura being developed for the market, provided I was able to source the most compatible casks that would enhance some of the spirit's rare flavours over time.

No matter what innovative styles may be created, everything relates back to wood, and it soon became apparent that a consistent wood management policy would have to be put in place. The casks in which Jura was being matured varied considerably in quality, with the result that much of the spirit was lacking body and charm. But there were exceptions, and, when it was good, Jura was very good indeed, especially in the older expressions. I wanted to increase the body, supported by warm, floral, buttery notes, and to do this for whiskies that would be bottled as our standard ten-year-old we began to vat and recask quantities of spirit in fresh, bourbon wood.

One of my prime objectives is to maintain the individual style of Jura. Delmé-Evans, who designed the current distillery in 1958, declared that he set out to produce spirit of a 'Highland character', but to me Jura is more specifically like a malt from the Spey valley. Many potential consumers jump to the erroneous conclusion that it is going to resemble an Islay whisky in style when they discover how close the distillery is to the 'whisky island'. What is not often taken into account is the great height and surface area of Jura's stills. They are some of the tallest in Scotland, which leads to a considerable degree of reflux.

If asked to describe the essential character of our ten-year-old Jura, I would say it has a zest, a tang of excitement about it. There is a freshness of sea spray, pine and gorse, balanced by a buttery, nutty, vanilla character that comes from the use of American white oak casks. But look out, too, for a seductive, flirtatious, floral side to it.

There is also a whisper of peat lurking in the background, which is not surprising as the island of Jura boasts significant peat deposits. It is considered unlucky on Jura to cut peats during the month of April, rather than May, as I learned one evening in the local bar. This set me thinking. Surely, the old Jura distillery of the nineteenth century would have produced heavily peated whiskies much like those of Islay? There was really no reason why we could not distill heavily peated whiskies once again. All we needed was a high phenol level in our malt. So we began distilling batches of heavily peated Jura in 1999. A number of different bottlings have been marketed as single malts, but the majority of this heavily peated spirit is used to create one of my favourite Jura expressions, Superstition.

What makes Superstition stand out from the rest of the Jura range is the complex phenolic aromas and flavours, which drift attractively in the background on the nose and palate. Additionally, notes of honey and marzipan are contributed by the 21-year-old Jura spirit included in the whisky's overall composition.

People often ask me about the best way to enjoy whisky, and I always reply that it depends very much on mood and circumstances. But for me, many whiskies are at their very best when drunk in the open air, Superstition particularly. The combination of peaty, spicy whisky which has spent long years in wood and the cold, biting wind and sea spray that so often characterise the Jura landscape make perfect partners. However, when it comes to luxury, a time to relax and enjoy a great dram with good friends, then Jura 16-year-old cannot be beaten. Immediately this noble spirit draws you into its hidden beauty with its warm and inviting flavours of marmalade, cinnamon and spiced honey with whispers of mint tea. If held long in the mouth, the warmth of the tongue will help to release many other hidden treasures. It is not surprising that this is the island's favourite aged single malt. I certainly will not argue with that!

There is something magical about the Isle of Jura. Often, when I am sitting in a noisy, bustling airport terminal waiting for a flight to Tokyo, Sydney or San Francisco, I long to feel the fresh, clean air of Small Isles Bay blowing gently across my face. To be able to work with the distillery staff, the people of the island, and one of the great malt whiskies – in such a setting – is one of the great pleasures of my professional life.

Extracted from *Goodness Nose: The Passionate Revelations of a Scotch Whisky Master Blender* by Richard Paterson and Gavin D Smith. Published by the Angels' Share, ISBN 978 1 903238 67 7, £19.99, www.nwp.co.uk.

Some Things I Covet in Jura Lodge

LIZ LOCHHEAD

that fearsomely fantastical
armchair upstairs made entirely of antlers and deerhide
   like something out of Cocteau's *La Belle et La Bête*
the tinpot suit of armour
the little green chipped 1940s kitchen chairs
the lobster creel for a lampshade
the pink teacup the typewriter the old black phone
the old scuffed leather sofa the red Paisley throw
the floral lining of the Edwardian cabin trunk in the
   Rose Room
the Mozart printed cushions in the Music Room
that big mad portrait in the Portrait Room
of some little plumed Lord Fauntleroy riding on a goat!
the tall French mirror in the Portrait Room
the huge shell in the White Room
the bluebirds
on the glass fingerplate in the Bluebird Room
the tipsy wooden sea-gull
on the bedside table in the Bluebird Room
the Victorian ladies' hunting jacket
the American Folk Art hangers with the heart-shaped
   cut-outs
the tall window in the hall
on the blue wall
with the perfectly framed view of one of the Paps

Biographies

JOHN BURNSIDE

John Burnside's first collection of poetry was published in 1988 and won a Scottish Arts Council Book Award. A later collection, *Feast Days*, won the Geoffrey Faber Memorial Prize, and *The Asylum Dance* was awarded the Whitbread Poetry Award. Since 1996 he has also written prose works, including novels, short stories and a memoir, *A Lie About My Father*. His two latest novels are *The Devil's Footprints* and *Glister*. He teaches Creative Writing at St Andrews University.

SIR BERNARD CRICK (1929–2008)

Sir Bernard Crick was Professor of Politics at Birkbeck College and knighted in 2001 for 'services to citizenship and political studies'. His best known books are *In Defence of Politics* and *George Orwell: A Life*. He visited Jura several times while writing the biography, then for the BBC Arena *Life of Orwell* film in 1984 and the BBC Scotland film *The Crystal Spirit*. He founded the George Orwell Prize for Political Writing.

DAVID FAITHFULL

David Faithfull studied at Duncan of Jordanstone College of Art and Design. Now based in Edinburgh, he lectures at the University of Dundee. Much of his work involves his relationship with the natural environment, and he has exhibited extensively, both nationally and internationally, with work in collections including the Tate, the Hunterian and the Scottish National Gallery of Modern Art.

JANICE GALLOWAY

Janice Galloway is the author of three award-winning novels, *The Trick Is To Keep Breathing*, *Foreign Parts* and *Clara*, plus two collections of short stories, *Blood* and *Where You Find It*. Her most recent book is the acclaimed memoir, *This Is Not About Me*. She has also collaborated on an opera libretto, *Monster*, based on the life of Mary Shelley, and with visual artist Anne Bevan on *Rosengarten*, a text and sculpture exhibition.

PHILIP GOUREVITCH

Philip Gourevitch is editor of the renowned literary magazine, *The Paris Review*, and author of an award-winning book on the Rwandan massacres, *We Wish To Inform You That Tomorrow We Will Be Killed With Our Families: Stories From Rwanda* (1998). He is a staff writer on *The New Yorker* and has reported from Cambodia, Burundi and Siberia. In 2001 he published *A Cold Case*, a true tale of crime and punishment in 1970s Manhattan, and in 2008, *Standard Operating Procedure*, which documents and analyses the Abu Ghraib prison scandal.

ROMESH GUNESEKERA

Born in Sri Lanka in 1954 Romesh has lived and worked in Britain since 1971. His first novel, *Reef,* was shortlisted for the Booker Prize in 1994 and the Guardian Fiction Prize. His second, *The Sandglass,* received the BBC's inaugural Asia Award for Writing and Literature and his third, *Heaven's Edge,* like his collection of short stories, *Monkfish Moon,* was a *New York Times* Notable Book of the Year. In 2005 he received a National Honour for his writing from Sri Lanka, and was elected a Fellow of the Royal Society of Literature in London. His most recent novel is *The Match.*

KATHLEEN JAMIE

Described in *Poetry Review* as 'a poetic voice of international significance', Kathleen studied philosophy at the University of Edinburgh. Her books, which include *The Tree House, Mr and Mrs Scotland Are Dead* and *Jizzen,* have been shortlisted for and won several prestigious literary awards. Her latest poetry collection, *The Tree House,* won the 2004 Forward Poetry Prize and the 2005 Scottish Arts Council Book of the Year Award. Her book of essays, *Findings,* won a Scottish Arts Council Book of the Year Award in 2006.

LIZ LOCHHEAD

Liz Lochhead's stage plays include *Blood and Ice, Mary Queen of Scots Got Her Head Chopped Off, Britannia Rules, Good Things, Perfect Days* and three rhyming versions from Molière, *Tartuffe*, Miseryguts (*Le Misanthrope*) and Educating Agnes (*L'Ecole des Femmes*); her adaptation of Euripides' *Medea* for Theatre Babel won the Saltire Society Scottish Book of the Year Award in 2001. Her poetry collections include *Dreaming Frankenstein* and *The Colour of Black & White* as well as the collection of monologues, lyrics and performance pieces, *True Confessions*, all published by Polygon. She was a recipient of a Cholmondley Award for Poetry, is a Fellow of Glasgow School of Art and was appointed Glasgow's Poet Laureate in 2005.

SWETHA PRAKASH

After moving to the UK from India in 2007, Swetha won the Charles Wallace India Trust Award to attend the creative writing programme at the Scottish Universities International Summer School at the University of Edinburgh. She is currently doing her MA in Writing at the University of Warwick where she is being tutored by A L Kennedy.

WILL SELF

Will is the author of four short-story collections, *The Quantity Theory of Insanity* (winner of the 1992 Geoffrey Faber award), *Grey Area, Tough Tough Toys for Tough Tough Boys* and most recently *Liver: A Fictional Organ with a Surface Anatomy of Four Lobes*; two novellas, *Cock and Bull* and *The Sweet Smell of Psychosis*; and five novels, *My Idea of Fun, Great Apes, How the Dead Live, The Book of Dave* and *The Butt*. He also writes for a plethora of publications and is a regular broadcaster on television and radio.

Acknowledgements

The editor would like to thank:

The people of Jura, always kind and welcoming.

Catriona Mack and the Isle of Jura Distillery staff, all of whom have been unfailingly helpful and generous with their time.

All at Whyte & Mackay, especially Philip McTeer, Cara Laing, John Douglas, Willie Tait, Richard Paterson, Sue Pettit and Willie Cochrane.

Neil Wilson for his generous permission to use an extract from Richard Paterson's *Goodness Nose*.

Arts & Business Scotland for their generous support.

Sophie Moxon, Sophy Dale, Jeanette Harris, Olivier Joly and Caitrin Armstrong at Scottish Book Trust.

Di Speirs and Elizabeth Allard at BBC Radio 4.

Alison Rae, Neville Moir, Hugh Andrew, Kenny Redpath, Jan Rutherford and James Hutcheson at Polygon/Birlinn.

The writers and artists involved: John Burnside, Janice Galloway, Philip Gourevitch, Romesh Gunesekera, Kathleen Jamie, Liz Lochhead, Swetha Prakash, Will Self, Charles MacLean, Alasdair Gray and David Faithfull.